Keeping Time

Jan 7, 2020
Dear Clint
Thank you for your
help from Luverne)
and Worthington)
yours truly)
John

Windmill of Wijk bij Duurstede, Jacob van Ruisdael, 1670

KEEPING TIME:

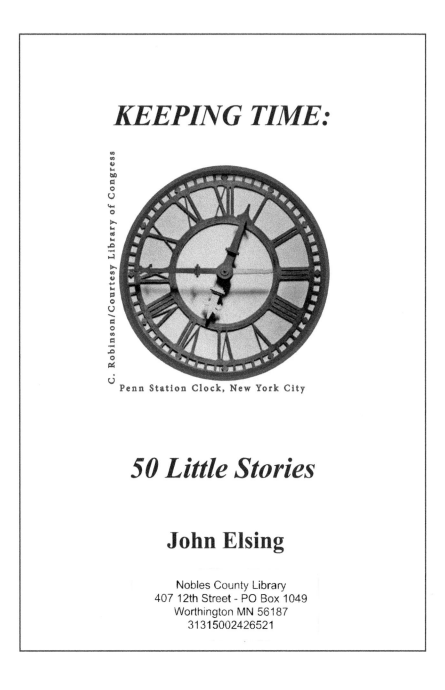

Penn Station Clock, New York City

50 Little Stories

John Elsing

Elsing, John
Keeping Time: 50 Little Stories

ISBN-13: 978-1546763956
ISBN-10: 1546763953

Editors: Kaaren Holum & Scott Lehmann
Book Layout & Design: Peter J. O'Toole
Copy Editing: Kathy Ollivier
Editorial Advisor: Jerry Swenson
Proofreader: Paul Picard
Team Leader: Shawn Hollembeak
Development Coordinator: Tim Schultz

The use of images in this book was done with guidance from the Code of Best Practices in Fair Use for the Visual Arts.

Printed in the United States of America

Courtesy innogy

Wind Turbines

Keeping Time: 70 Little Stories (2012)

Foreword

Writing a story can be likened to painting a picture or composing music. It comes from within. Diane Thome, American composer and first woman to receive a Ph.D. in music from Princeton, told me she began composing in elementary school because she could not say no to her powerful need to make music. It took a long time before anything like that happened to me.

Like Grandma Moses and painting, I was not young when I started writing in earnest. One morning in May of my 70th year, I sat down and wrote my first story. It was short, but I knew at the time it would not be my last. I wanted to keep going. There was nothing on my calendar that needed immediate attention, so the writing continued. Six months later, there were rough drafts for more than a hundred stories, 70 of which you can find in *Keeping Time: 70 Little Stories*, published by CreateSpace, a division of Amazon, in 2012.

After that, several years passed in which I did not write anything. During that time, I remember thinking there would be no more stories, but I did not worry about it. And then, on a cold winter day, it happened again. Instead of writing to a friend, I found myself writing a story. Quite a surprise. When it was finished, I wrote another, and then another. When spring arrived that year, there were several dozen new stories on my desk. Fifty of them are included in this book.

John Elsing
Minneapolis
2016

Storytelling

Tell Me a Story

Ever since people first gathered around stick fires in caves, storytelling has been part of the human experience. Across continents and cultures, it has continued unbroken through the centuries to the present time of high tech.

Why is this so?

Storytelling brings people together. It meets a need we all have to be part of the whole, to be connected to something larger than ourselves.

How are stories created?

In ancient times people made up stories and shared them with one another. As time went by, some of these stories were remembered and passed down from one generation to the next. Some of them are still with us today.

How do stories get written?

Writing today is big business, but anyone can write a story. It is relatively easy for some people, more difficult for others. Some writers are paid for their work. The rest can pay companies to make their books for them.

What is writing?

Professors at writing workshops can teach their students how to make sentences, but no one can teach others what to say. People have to figure that out for themselves.

Explanation

The 50 stories in this book are based on events that touched my life and the lives of people I knew, but this is not a history book. It is, first and foremost, a storybook. I used my imagination to complete it.

Throughout my life, I've heard relatives and friends give varying accounts of many events mentioned here, but when it came time to write these stories, I found gaps in the information available to me. When memory failed, I tried to fill in the blanks as faithfully as I could, always hoping to retain the integrity of what I had heard, while at the same time paying respect to those whose stories these are. For privacy's sake, the names of some people and places have been changed.

The stories begin in Holland in the late 1800s, when my paternal grandmother, Effie Ameland (not her real name), was thirteen years old. That was more than 50 years before I was born. They end with a story I began writing for my granddaughter when we were in Paris in the summer of 2015. She was ten years old, and I was three years from 80.

Although the stories are arranged in rough chronological fashion, they do not comprise a seamless narrative. On the contrary, most of the stories can stand alone. They are meant to be shared and read aloud as single stories in whatever order you wish. Readers are encouraged to check the Table of Contents and begin with titles that might interest them.

Keeping Time: 50 Little Stories (2016) is not all sweetness and light. Far from it. Unlike *Keeping Time: 70 Little Stories* (2012), some of the stories included here are sad and not always suitable for children.

Here are the names of the major players:

Who's Who

The four Elsing brothers
    Ben, George, John, Sam

Effie Ameland and Sam Elsing
    My paternal grandparents

Effie and Sam's children
    John, Henry, Herman (my dad), Annie, Etta

Grandma and Grandpa Fischer
    My maternal grandparents

Grandma and Grandpa's children
    Lena, Jennie, Clara, Lillie, Mary (my mother), and two boys who died in early childhood

Marie
    My sister, whom we called Sister, or Little Sister

Gramma Hardy
    A close friend of our family

Dirk Hardy
    Gramma's son

"The universe is made of stories, not of atoms."
—Muriel Rukeyser, *The Speed of Darkness* (1968)

Table of Contents

Part Two
1950–2015

Hourglass

Keeping Time

Not possessing Proustian gifts,
one forgets,
little by little,
what long-ago times were like.

Today,
as I look back
and try to remember,
I can only catch glimpses of the way we were.

Now and again
a detail
or two
will stand out.

Something takes one's attention for a minute,
but then it,
too,
slips away,
back into the blur.

One makes an effort to get what has gone before to stand still,
the better to observe it,
but it wriggles and jiggles and escapes our grasp,
precluding closer examination.

Occasionally one can recall times when the moving finger
stopped
for a moment,
but when one catches up,
it has moved on,
closer to the edge of oblivion.
Try though we do to capture it,
the past keeps slipping away – until we find that we can regard a
year,
or more,
without so much as a sentence comment.

Although our bodies cannot,
our memories can,
almost magically,
leap over mountains of time
until we find ourselves facing that second vast eternity.

John Elsing

Rooster

4

Eternal Vigilance

Just as farms on the American prairie were once notable for their barbed-wire fences, the polders in Holland are famous for their dikes, some of which are not always in good repair. Sometimes in the cool of an evening, people in the Netherlands walk out to look at the dikes, just as Midwestern farmers once checked their fences. That was before modern farming practices rendered fences obsolete in many parts of the United States.

In the days before cars and television sets, whole families would go walking together to check on things around them, whether down the street or out in the field. Nowadays, with ever more technological marvels to amuse us, scenes of this kind are no longer common, but along the shores of the North Sea, people still pay careful attention to the condition of the dikes.

For historical reasons like the Northwest Ordinance of 1787 and the Homestead Act of 1862, farmsteads in America are scattered across the landscape, isolated from one another. In many parts of Europe, however, country people live together in villages. Because Holland is one of the most densely populated places on the planet, one finds a multitude of villages there. They are so close together that, as the sun rises slowly in the east, roosters crowing in eastern villages wake people in villages to the west before the sun is high enough to shine directly into the windows of their houses.

My paternal grandmother, Effie, loved her village, and one of the things she liked about it was being able to walk out onto the dikes, either alone or with others. Her parents did not have to worry about her tumbling into water because from her village, for most of the year, there was no water to be seen in any direction. That did not mean that people could stop worrying about the sea. Whenever storms brought a lot of rain in a short period of time, weather conditions could change dramatically. People who live on land that lies below sea level can never quite forget that even though there might be many dikes between one's home and the sea, the water can still come rushing in, faster than a horse can run, and earthen dikes can be washed away. Today a large and formidable network of defenses designed to hold back the sea protects the country, but it can never be enough.

So, when Effie went walking with her family and friends, they never forgot to look to the dikes. They knew the importance of a good dike master. If they neglected the upkeep of the dikes, they did so at their peril; for that reason, they paid attention to small signs. Bitter experience had taught them that danger lurks in the details, and that calculated watchfulness can save lives.

Dutch Houses, Earthen Dike

Bremen Ship

Crossing the Atlantic

I.   Ameland Family

For as long as my paternal grandmother Effie could remember, her parents had been planning to immigrate to America, to Minnesota. Effie was thirteen years old in 1892 when she crossed the Atlantic Ocean with her family. The voyage took almost two weeks. Effie remembered walking from one end of the ship to the other in the early morning hours with a neighbor girl, but they had to be careful. The fresh air was pleasant, but watching burial at sea was not. That's why it was done when the ship's crew thought no one was watching.

Burial happened quickly and without ceremony. The dead were wrapped in sheets, and stretcher-bearers brought them to the railing. Two men put the stretcher down on the deck, with the foot end pointing out toward the water. Then they moved to the head end of the stretcher, upended it, and the body slid off and went over the side. Sometimes a sheet flapped in the breeze. The girls always listened for the splash, but they never heard it.

At Ellis Island, Effie feared being separated from her family, but the name-tag system worked well, and the people helping the new arrivals were brisk and efficient. A wagon with the word "society" lettered on its side carried them to their lodgings. A few days later it returned and took them to a train that would go all the way to Chicago, where they were met early in the morning by people who spoke their language. The Amelands spent the nights in a church dormitory, and during the day they bought what they needed for the next leg of the trip west.

USA North Central States

II. Elsing Brothers

From the time they were children, the four Elsing boys had never been able to agree on much of anything, but when the opportunity for immigrating to the United States presented itself, the Four Dutchmen, as they were often called, decided to cross the Atlantic together.

The ocean voyage was difficult. Traveling by train from New York to Chicago and then on to Worthington, Minnesota, which was as far as the railroad went at that time, was worse.

Train Depot, Worthington, 1898

Passenger Train, 1898

Train Wreck

When the immigrants left Chicago, they were followed by freight trains filled with animals, machinery, furniture, and provisions of all kinds. By the time the Ameland family and the Elsing brothers neared the Minnesota border, there were just two smaller trains, one for passengers and one for freight. Later it was said that the freight train had not left enough room between itself and the passenger train, and the combined weight of the two trains traveling so close together caused part of the railroad embankment to collapse. The passenger train got across safely, but the freight train derailed and caught fire.

My paternal grandfather, Sam, and his brothers lost almost everything they had brought with them from Holland and Chicago. They arrived in Worthington with just their hand luggage and the clothes they were wearing. Decisions had to be made. The four young men understood themselves well enough to know that consequences of what happened next would echo through the generations and far into the future.

As usual, the brothers disagreed on how to proceed. Three of them – George, John, and Sam – chose to continue west out to the little hills of the prairie[*] on the west slope of Buffalo Ridge in Nobles County. The fourth brother, Ben, opted to take his portion of their patrimony and boarded a train going east. He settled in Cottonwood County, alone.

It was not an easy decision for them to make – no decision ever was, it seemed – but the brothers parted on good terms and made a promise to their parents which they kept for more than a quarter century, namely, to stay in touch with one another and be ready to help should help be needed.

* * * * * * *

My grandmother's family, the Amelands, had relatives in Nobles County. When they heard of the catastrophic event that had befallen the Elsing brothers, they offered to take them in, and even though times were hard, they helped in any way they could until the brothers were able to get themselves established.

That was how the Ameland and Elsing families met.

---

[*] The early French explorers called this part of the Upper Midwest the *Coteaux des Prairies*.

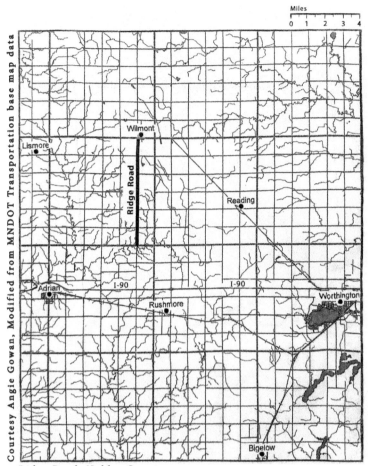

Ridge Road, Nobles County

15

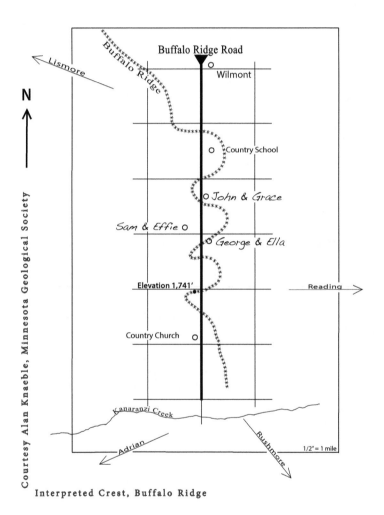

N

Buffalo Ridge Road

Lismore

Buffalo Ridge

Wilmont

Country School

John & Grace

Sam & Effie

George & Ella

Elevation 1,741'

Reading

Country Church

Kanaranzi Creek

Adrian

Rushmore

1/2" = 1 mile

Courtesy Alan Knaeble, Minnesota Geological Society

Interpreted Crest, Buffalo Ridge

Ridge Road

The three Nobles County brothers left Worthington and followed the historic Native American trail along Buffalo Ridge to the northwest. There is a break in the ridge at the Reading crossing, and here the brothers turned and went straight west for six miles. They were nearing the Ameland family farms, where they planned to stay until they could buy land of their own.

Here, at one of the highest elevations in the county – 1,741 feet – they came to Ridge Road.[*] From this point they could see the small towns of Reading, Rushmore, Adrian, and Lismore, none of them more than ten miles away. Kanaranzi Creek was two miles south of this intersection, and the town of Wilmont was four miles away to the north, but they could not see it because Buffalo Ridge blocks the view of the town from where the brothers were standing.

The brothers could not know it at the time, but their lives would unfold along the six miles of Ridge Road from Kanaranzi Creek north to Wilmont. All three of them bought land along the middle two miles of this road: John and George on the east side, Sam on the west. The farms of John and George were on the ridge crest.

---

[*] This road crosses the crest of Buffalo Ridge seven times between Wilmont and Kanaranzi Creek (United States Department of the Interior Geological Survey, Adrian NE Quadrangle, Minnesota-Nobles County, 1965).

Sam's farmland started a hundred yards away from the crest line, on the west side of the road.

The three brothers had made a pact to stay together, and it was about to become a reality. When the wind was blowing in the right direction, the young farmers were almost within shouting distance of one another. George and Sam's farm buildings were less than half a mile apart. John's buildings were a little over half a mile from those of his brothers.

As the years passed, the three brothers prospered, and they welcomed news that arrived from time to time saying the same was true for their brother Ben.

Courtesy Peter J. O'Toole

Ridge Road

Basilica Barn

20

Blue Barns

In the early 1900s, there were almost a dozen large buildings on the three Elsing farms south of Wilmont, Minnesota. Most of them had gambrel roofs. Ella and George Elsing's barn was the exception to the family predilection for this type of roof.

Aunt Ella had distant relatives in Italy and knew a lot about that country. She liked the basilica plan used in many of its churches, and so did George. The basilica plan has a long, two-story rectangular center section – the nave – and enclosed porches on both of the long sides.

Emmanuel Masqueray, a French architect, was chosen by Archbishop John Ireland of St. Paul to guide the construction of the Basilica of St. Mary in Minneapolis. Masqueray went to Italy to make plans for it. Ella and George were interested in Masqueray's work. They had hoped one day to build a basilica church, but there was already a church in their Nobles County community, so they abandoned that idea. However, when they saw that their farm was located on one of the highest elevations of Buffalo Ridge and enjoyed views in all directions – like the biblical city on the hill – they decided to use the basilica plan for their barn.

They placed it precisely on the highest acre of the northwest

NOBLES COUNTY COURTHOUSE
WORTHINGTON, MINNESOTA

Nobles County Courthouse, Worthington

corner of their 160-acre farm. Hundreds of barns in the Upper Midwest and throughout the country can trace their origins to the basilicas of ancient Rome, but their owners are often not aware of this connection.

There were only a few basilica barns in Nobles County at that time. The locals regarded them with interest, as something different, but not otherwise remarkable. What made Ella's barn the talk of the county was the fact that she painted it and its ensemble buildings a light blue. It was an unusual color for farm buildings, most of which were red and white, but I don't think it was without precedent. One of them may have inspired Helen Sewell's book, *Blue Barns*, which she wrote more than twenty years later, in the 1930s. It was one of my favorite books when I was in grade school. Its pictures showed the only other set of blue buildings I have ever seen on a farm.

Before the trees grew up around it, the barn could be seen from the small towns spread across the surrounding countryside, and at night, from the barn's high windows, one could see the revolving beacon in the tower of the Nobles County Courthouse in Worthington, fifteen miles to the southeast.

Ella and George were proud of their farm with its basilica barn on Buffalo Ridge. Dad's family dressed in their Sunday best when they went up the hill to visit them. They always took the buggy, never the wagon, because Ella and George liked things to be nice. Ella was elegant, and George was tall and handsome. My grandmother Effie taught her girls to curtsy for their aunt and reminded the boys to be sure their jackets were buttoned and their trousers bloused. Then she added, "And don't forget to nod your heads when you take your caps off."

Ella was my father's favorite aunt. We were in Canada when she passed away in 1947. There was no way we could get back in time for her funeral. Dad always regretted not having been at home for that service.

Ella kept a large garden and took pleasure in the orchard and the lawn around it. When the weather was mild, she liked to sit out there and watch the ducks in the seasonal pond across the road. She often wished she could have a water garden with lilies over there, but it wasn't her land. It wasn't our land either, but when Dad was a boy he sometimes pretended the pond was a rice paddy. Instead of planting rice in it, he planted water lilies for his aunt, but he was shy and never told her that. When he became a man, he farmed the wetland across the road from her house for more than twenty years. In the spring, he left the pond for Aunt Ella's ducks. Every year he looked forward to seeing them return for a few days.

* * * * * * * *

Aunt Ella's visitors always sat in the parlor where everything had its place. She wore her long black dress with the high starched collar and an amber necklace. No one ever told Dad she was a countess.

One Sunday afternoon, the older girls made the tea and served it. The middle girl passed the cookies around when it was time for the second cup. When she came to Dad, there were only two cookies left on the plate. One was larger than the other. Dad looked at them, decided that being polite had its limits, and took the larger one. His cousin, Jeanette, said, "If the plate were being passed to me, I would take the smaller cookie." Dad looked at her and said, "Well, the smaller cookie is right there, so you can still have it."

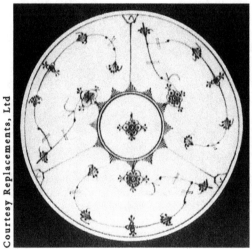

"Blue Lines and Flowers on White," Porsgrund

President Theodore Roosevelt

Theodore Roosevelt

The old-timers in Rushmore, Minnesota, could remember the day – September 3, 1910 – when Theodore Roosevelt's train stopped in town, and he spoke to the crowd. Dad remembered the big, yellowing pictures of Roosevelt that used to hang in the depot waiting room.

Roosevelt was a commanding figure. He had overcome adversity and left his mark on the nation. Those who heard him speak that day knew that both his mother and his wife had died on the same day years before this visit, and that he had been left to raise his daughter, Alice, without them. This double loss was a heavy blow for Roosevelt, and people feared it might be the end of him. Instead of giving up, however, he moved to what had been the Dakota Territory, which began less than 40 miles west of the little town of Rushmore. Out there on his ranch, alongside the cowhands, he worked hard, built himself up, and slowly put his life back together.

Years later, when the residents of Rushmore read Ole Rölvaag's *Giants in the Earth*, they remembered Teddy Roosevelt and the larger-than-life impression he had made on them that day.

The people who settled in Nobles County were acquainted with hardship. They knew pioneers like the woman in Rölvaag's

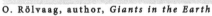

O. Rölvaag, author, *Giants in the Earth*

Minnesota Historical Society

book who crawled out of her family's covered wagon, looked at the prairie landscape around her, and said, "There isn't even a tree to hide behind."

The early settlers knew what it was like being out in the middle of nowhere, on the highest elevations of Buffalo Ridge, where the wind was always strongest, with nothing but the stars to guide them. And when the stars were obscured, it was so dark that people found it difficult to stand up, sometimes lost their balance, and fell over.

But there were compensations, too. Some of those who came from the east turned around and went back, but others found the grandeur of the prairie to their liking and came to cherish the land, as Roosevelt had. They loved the northern lights and sometimes tumbled out of bed in the dark of night to watch those great shafts of pale, sorbet-colored light gyrate in the northern sky. Sometimes whole families wrapped themselves in blankets, took their kitchen chairs outside and marveled at what the Lord had made. After a while, they went back to bed and recovered sleep. It may be that the spectacular show gave them the strength they needed to face another day of hard work.

New High Water Mark at Power House.
June 13, 1914.

Courtesy Lakesnwoods.com

Luverne, Minnesota, 1914

Champepedan Creek
June 13, 1914

Try to imagine a single large oak tree out in the middle of the rolling prairie. The wind blows hard in southwestern Minnesota, and the tree has struggled mightily to survive the harsh climate on the west slope of Buffalo Ridge. All its branches are gnarled, but the people who live in this part of the country consider oak trees to be beautiful, especially in winter when they are dusted with snow.

Now imagine you have taken a black-and-white photo of this tree, and you are pressing it flat on a page in your scrapbook. What you see will look rather like a drawing of the Rock River Major Watershed. The branches of the tree represent creeks and streams, and they carry their water down to the base of the tree trunk at Luverne.[*]

The small town of Kenneth is ten miles northeast of Luverne. The farm where mother's Uncle John and his family lived during the first half of the twentieth century is out on the bluff east of town, above the broad Champepedan Creek valley. We visited there when I was a boy. It was less than a dozen miles west of our farm.

Two things in particular have stayed with me through all

---

[*] On June 17, 2014, the Rock River crested at 16.85 feet above flood stage in Luverne, Minnesota, the highest ever. On June 13, 1914, it crested at 14.10, the third highest ever.

the years since then. The first is the Carrara marble countertop in the butcher shop in Kenneth, where our relatives had a cold storage locker. I had seen pictures of statues carved from Carrara marble, but I had never touched marble before. It was beautiful, and I liked running my fingers over it. Every time someone went into town, I asked if they were going to stop at the butcher shop, and would they mind taking me along. One day Uncle John called me "the Carrara kid," and from then on, whenever we visited, everybody called me that.

* * * * * * * *

The second memory is a story Uncle John told me. The two of us were sitting on the bench in his kitchen garden overlooking the valley, and he was painting a picture called "Landscape with Barn." The barn in that painting did not look like other barns I'd seen.

"Where did you find that barn?" I asked.

Uncle said it was a mountain barn in the Austrian Tyrol. Later that afternoon, he finished the painting and gave it to me to keep.

The buildings on Uncle John's farm were not arranged like most farm buildings. They sat high on the bluff overlooking the Champepedan Valley. Champepedan Creek came down from the north and disappeared out to the south. The valley floor started at the foot of the bluff, two hundred yards down the slope in front of us. The white farm house was a city block north, to our left, and the red barn, larger even than ours, was to our right. The valley lay in front of us, to the east. Behind us there was a thick grove of cottonwood trees.

A stream ran through the vegetable garden down to the floor of the valley. Uncle John planted his garden around a series of pools in the stream; when he wanted to water a section of the garden, he placed shingles in the channel so its pool overflowed. The first time we saw it, Mother called the idea ingenious. For a long time after that, I called everything I liked "ingenious."

Years later, on the University of Colorado campus in Boulder, I saw irrigation ditches that could be closed off by placing a block of wood in them, causing the ditches to overflow and water the grass in one or another part of the campus lawn. "Ah, ingenious," I said to myself.

Looking out from the garden, we could see weather-ravaged trees straggling along a fence line. Uncle John sat quietly for a while, then took up his brushes and added dabs of paint here and there to the painting. When he finished, he told me what had happened in the valley on June 13, 1914, almost forty years earlier:

"The sky was battleship gray that morning. While we were having lunch, it rained hard, and it continued raining off and on throughout the early afternoon. We noticed that the creek winding through the valley had begun to overflow its banks.

"It was the kind of rain that didn't seem likely to stop anytime soon. I put on my slicker and my volunteer fireman's hood and walked out on the lawn. I stopped to throw the switch that prevented water from entering the garden and sent it down the side channel instead, over the edge of the bluff, not like a waterfall, but flowing rapidly. As I turned to go on to the barn, I looked out to my left and saw there was now a lot of water flowing outside the creek bed. That worried me. On my way back to the house I noticed a small herd of cattle sheltering among the trees along the fence line in the valley. Some of them were having trouble making their way through the water, and the calves were swimming. At the edge of the bluff, I took off my hood and began waving it to my right, hoping to get the animals to go in that direction, where it would have been easier for them to get out of the water and onto higher ground. The grade directly below me was too steep for that.

"And then, like an echo from far away, I heard a shout followed by another, and another. I looked out through the rain and saw my neighbor on horseback. He was waving his hat back and forth, attempting to get the animals to turn, just as I had been trying to do.

"The rider and his horse, and most of the cattle, were less than a quarter mile away; some of them were closer. I tried to signal him, but without success. He did not see me. The rain slacked off a little, and I looked farther to the north. I could not believe my eyes. There was a dam farther up in the Chanarambie Valley, and I thought for a moment it might have given way. A wall of water was coming down from the north, flooding the valley floor. The only thing visible behind the surging water was more water: no trees, no animals, no fences, nothing, just a vast expanse of roiling water.

"I flailed my arms about and shouted, trying to warn my friend, but he wasn't looking in my direction. He was still trying to get the cattle to move downstream. I knew it was too late for that. Horror gripped me as I realized he was going to be overtaken by the water bearing down on him. He should try to get himself and his horse out of the current and over to higher ground, I thought, but he continued as before. He did not see the water coming up behind him.

"The crest had almost reached him before he turned and saw it for the first time. He tried to rein his horse to the right and move toward the bluff, but the current was too strong. It was too late. The water overwhelmed him. His horse was in trouble; it had lost its footing and was trying to swim for shore, but it could only thrash about and was making no headway at all. The raging water took both horse and rider under, and for a few seconds they both disappeared from view. They reappeared and seemed to recover themselves a little, but then an even bigger wave covered them completely. They disappeared again. By this time, all the smaller animals and many of the others were gone. The ones remaining were caught in the churning water. The horse and its rider popped up once more, and then they, too, were lost."

Des Moines River

After the War was Over

One August weekend the fourth Elsing brother, Ben, took his family to visit their relatives in Nobles County, where he had arrived years earlier with his three brothers. The family traveled by horse and buggy from near Windom, on the Des Moines River, to his brother Sam's place on the west slope of Buffalo Ridge.

By now Sam Elsing and Effie Ameland had been married for more than twenty years. Effie's unmarried brother, Henry, was living with them. Henry had fought in France during the Great War and, as a result of injuries sustained in the fighting there, had been hospitalized for a long time in England. He was an outspoken young man, and his family had known for a long time that he was the opposite of slow to anger.

When families went to visit one another in those days, it was usual for them to stay overnight with their relatives. Horses could not be expected to go from one county far into the next and then back again, all in the same day.

It was after ten o'clock in the evening, and the two Dutch families were having their last cup of tea for the day when the subject of the war came up for discussion. Later, it was generally agreed that Ben, the Cottonwood County brother, had not said anything offensive. On the contrary, it could have been regarded as perfectly innocuous, but Effie's brother chose not to let it pass unremarked. Unfortunately for all concerned, he made an issue of it and said, "Oh well, you always did favor the Germans."

Ben took serious offense at this remark. He stood up and said, "Boys, go out to the barn and harness the horses; we're going home."

Dutch people tend to be taciturn and are not in the habit of saying much when push comes to shove. No one remembered if anything at all was said after this. The horses and buggy were brought to the front gate. Ben and his family left on a long night's journey over unimproved roads without street lights to guide them.

None of the three Nobles County brothers ever saw him again.

* * * * * * * *

One Sunday afternoon in the 1960s, long after all four brothers were dead, our family went to visit one of Dad's cousins in Cottonwood County. The visit was nice enough, but by then, too much time had passed, and it was too late to put things right.

The Great War

Plow Pulled by Horses

Rosemary of Scotland

All the Samenfelder women were strong, tall, and capable. Their brothers were like them, except for one difference: they were not blessed with long lives. Already as young men, two of the three Minnesota brothers were advised to leave the Upper Midwest because of health problems. They were lucky, however, to marry women who were much like their sisters, and that may explain why the family has flourished for more than a hundred years. You can find their descendants in more than half a dozen states on both sides of the Mississippi River. They possessed a gift that enabled them to bloom where they were planted, but they also had the wit to do some research before they attempted to put down roots.

The first brother, Albert, moved to the high plains of eastern Colorado because the land was cheap, and there was a lot of it. He was asthmatic, and the dry climate proved to be salutary for his troubles.

The second brother, Robert, pulled up stakes and moved with his wife, Rosemary, and their children to Salem, Oregon. When Rosemary, a Scotswoman, was told that the doctor had suggested they move to Oregon because of Robert's allergies, she said, "Well, when I married Robert, I had never heard of Minnesota, so as long as I've come this far with him, I don't see any reason why I should not keep going, if that's what the doctor says is best." And then she added, "By the way, where exactly is Salem, Oregon?"

The family took everything they owned with them on the train: household goods and animals, as well as machinery. Only a few months after they settled in Salem, Robert died, leaving Rosemary with small children and debts. She didn't look back. Instead, she put her hand to the plow they had brought with them from Minnesota and started a new life for herself and her family.

One of the most vivid stories her descendants tell about her is how she stood up to an entire railway company. A widow with a large family and a farm to manage, she learned one day that a second railroad was coming to Salem. The owners were planning to lay tracks right across her land, effectively cutting it in half. She wrote to the company officers and told them she needed an underpass so her milk cows could go back and forth between the barn and the pasture. I don't know if it is true that the railroad people laughed, but they certainly did not take her seriously. Their surveyors appeared at the farm, went out to her fields and into the pasture without first seeking permission, and began pounding stakes. Rosemary appealed to officials in the City of Salem, people who could and should have helped her, but they did nothing. Left with no alternative, she had to fend for herself. Not one to be bullied by what she called the railroad's "high and mighty" tactics, she was determined to stand her ground.

On the day when the railroad's grading equipment appeared at her place, there she was, seated on her buckboard, flanked by her children, with her shotgun across her knees. She had taken the precaution of padlocking the gates to the property, thereby assuring that trespassing on it would be regarded as a more serious offense. Had it been common all those years ago to make movies about formidable women, her children always said they would have chosen Agnes Moorhead in a bonnet to play the part of their mother.

The railway people approached, asked her to remove the padlocks and allow them to pass so they could do what they had come to do. Rosemary could have fired off a round or two. They were, after all, trespassing, and it is well known that Americans have a sacred right to protect and defend their property, but she did not do that. She was not the kind of person who stoops to histrionics to make a point. No, she knew she had the law on her side, and it soon became apparent that the railroad people had met their match. To their credit, they left the same way they had arrived, quietly, and the next day they brought a contract for Rosemary to sign. It guaranteed an underpass – a very nice one as it turned out – and it didn't cost her a penny.

This young farmer's wife was clearly someone to be reckoned with. People admired her spirit and what she had accomplished. Dad said she should run for governor. Before she was forty, her friends and neighbors had elected her to the state legislature. By the time she was fifty, her name was known and respected throughout the state.

One day the principal of the school Rosemary's children had attended invited her to speak at an all-school assembly. It was a presidential election year. In his introductory remarks, the principal asked the young people, "Who's going to be the next president?" You could have heard a pin drop, and then, as if on cue, the audience stood as one and cheered: "Rosemary of Scotland!"

When she was an old woman and feminist voices were making themselves heard, Rosemary was often asked to give speeches. She always accepted, but she never made a speech; instead, she made it her habit to say to her listeners, "Just ask me anything you'd like to." As the years passed, dozens of people did just that, and one question in particular came up time and time again. Whenever Rosemary heard it coming, she would present a smile so beguiling that everyone in attendance smiled with her. Rosemary always repeated the question for the benefit of those who had perhaps not heard it the first time: "How did you get to the state legislature?" And after that she would reply, "Well, in my case, the capitol building was just a couple miles down the road from my farm, so I just walked." Her audiences loved it.

* * * * * * * *

Although Rosemary had married into the Samenfelder family, she proved herself to be more like her in-laws than they were themselves.

44

Courtesy www.theflagshop.co.uk

Flag of Scotland

Sam Elsing Farmhouse, c. 1914

Country Boy

My father, Herman, was a country boy. He was born in the downstairs bedroom of Sam and Effie's farmhouse in 1906, and he died in that room almost 75 years later. He was in his early 20s when he saw the Nobles County Courthouse for the first time.

His early life was spent along the six miles of Ridge Road* in Larkin Township. The small Catholic town of Wilmont was at the north end of the road. His grade school, District 84, was a mile and a half south of the town. The three Elsing farms bordered the third and fourth miles of the road, and the Dutch church stood at the end of the fifth mile.

From there the road went downhill to Kanaranzi Creek, where it dropped Ridge from its name. Now just a township road, it passed between the Thom and Ebeling farms before continuing on to the Protestant town of Rushmore, six miles away.

Herman was the third of five children. There were two older brothers, John and Henry, and two younger sisters, Annie and Etta. All four of his siblings did well in school, even though they spoke Dutch at home.

---

* Today there are hundreds of tall wind turbines on Buffalo Ridge in southwestern Minnesota.

47

From the very beginning, though, school was not easy for Herman. He learned English from an older classmate, Jennie, who would one day be his sister-in-law. She taught him well. I thought his English was accent-free, but my children said they could hear the trace of a Dutch accent in the way he pronounced some words. Any grammatical mistakes he made were negligible. He was quick at math and had a good sense of humor, but found it difficult to read and almost impossible to write. When he did write something, his penmanship was neat, but it took him a long time.

He almost certainly suffered from what is today called dyslexia, but back then, out in the country, no one knew what that was. Except for Jennie, people sometimes grew impatient with him. He found this frustrating and grew increasingly impatient with himself. Only once did he ever speak to me about his reading problem. He asked why is it that words keep moving off the page. Mother never mentioned his reading. It may be he never shared that with her.

We were sitting in big chairs in the bank lobby, waiting to transact business, the first time I realized something was wrong. Dad picked up a sheet of paper and slowly wrote his name on it. Then he asked me to write his name like that. My handwriting was Palmer method and his was spiky, but when he saw that I could imitate his handwriting well enough, he said our business would go faster if I signed for him. From then on, I went with him whenever his signature was needed.

PSALM 23

The Lord is my shepherd,
I shall not want.
He maketh me to lie down in
green pastures, he leadeth me beside
the still waters.
He restoreth my soul,
he leadeth me in the paths of
righteousness for his name's sake.
Yea, though I walk through the valley
of the shadow of death, I will
fear no evil, for thou art with me.
Thy rod and thy staff they comfort
me.
Thou preparest a table before
me in the presence of mine enemies.
Thou anointest my head with oil,
my cup runneth over.

Surely goodness and mercy shall
follow me all the days of my life,
and I will dwell in the house of
the Lord forever.

Dad fell in love with Mother when they were children. They met in Sunday school. She was six, and he was eleven. One Sunday the teacher asked Mary to read Psalm 23 aloud. Mary was one of the youngest children in the class, but she read with expression, and it was easy to understand her. Dad told me he knew then that he wanted to marry her, but she and her family moved to Rushmore soon after that and began attending the church on their street. Sometimes they drove out to the country church, but those times were few.

The years passed, and he never forgot the day he heard Mary read for the first time. He wanted to learn to read like that, and it must have been one of the reasons why he was attracted to her.

From time to time there was news of her, but that didn't happen very often. Her family lived in town now, but their farm bordered the far side of Uncle George's land, and sometimes Herman saw Mary's father at one or another of the Elsing places. Mary's father had a trucking company, and he sometimes drove a truck himself. Herman asked his mother to inquire about Mary, and his request was taken to heart. As the years passed, he learned that Mary and her sister, Lillie, were attending high school in Worthington. They boarded with friends of the family, the Stantons, during the week, and on weekends they took the train back to Rushmore to be with their parents. Herman also learned that Mary, like her older sister, was planning to become a teacher. He welcomed this news.

When Lillie finished high school, she took the two-year teacher-training course, received her teaching certificate, and found a job at a country school five miles north of Rushmore. After high school, Mary followed in her sister's footsteps and completed the two-year teacher-training program. That same year Lillie married and was obliged to give up her teaching job. Mary applied for the position and was hired. For Herman, this was like answered prayer, a dream come true. He had waited for more than a dozen years, during which he had seen Mary only a few times. Now she was teaching at a school just three miles away.

One day he "took his heart in his hands" and drove his horse and buggy over to the school in the late afternoon. He watched from the ridge as the children walked home to their farms, and then he continued on to the school.

Mary was just leaving the schoolhouse, ready to walk the half mile to her lodgings. Herman tied the horse and buggy to the rail and went up to the steps. Mary did not recognize him until he introduced himself, but then she remembered him. He asked if she would like a ride back to the place where she was rooming. She said she did not need a ride, but she thanked him, saying she appreciated the offer. He asked if he could stop by sometime the following week, and she said, "No, I don't think so."

He declared himself for her, and she said it dismayed her to hear it because she already had a beau. She asked him not to come calling again, but when she saw how deeply this rejection affected him, she said she hoped they could be friends. He thanked her, turned, and drove away.

* * * * * * * *

The next time Mary's father stopped at our farm, he stayed for afternoon tea, and my grandmother learned that Mary was engaged to be married to Dirk Hardy. Herman didn't say much when she told him. He got up, went outside, and started on the evening chores.

* * * * * * * *

In January, 1931, Dirk was driving from Rushmore out to the country school where Mary taught. There was snow on the ground and some ice on the road. As the car rounded the bend and started down the long hill to cross Kanaranzi Creek, it hit an icy patch, spun out of control, and tumbled down the steep embankment into the creek bed. Dirk was thrown from the vehicle. The car rolled over, and when it came to rest, he was crushed beneath it. He died before help could reach him.

Someone drove to Rushmore and told Lillie's husband, Bill, what had happened. Lillie and Bill drove out to the school together. Mary went back with them to her parents' house in town. Lillie substituted for her sister until after the funeral. The next month Mary returned to teaching.

During Lent, Herman drove over to the school house. He proposed marriage, Mary accepted, and they married in June. A few years later Mary suffered a miscarriage in the Slayton hospital. Lillie was staying with her. Bill and Herman were ticketed for speeding in Fulda on their way to get to them.

Mary and Herman tried for another child, but that was not to be. Seven years later they adopted me. It was January, 1939. I was eight months old.

Country Church

Shetland Pony

Nina

Nina Renselaar was the same age as Mother. They went to school together. Nina was a country girl, and Mother lived in Rushmore, but both were daughters of the prairie. The sun, the wind, and the rain were the same whether one had a house in town or a farm in the country.

Mother's family lived near the town schoolhouse. On school days, she went out to the front porch, or sat on the front steps, and waited for her friend Nina and her pony to appear on Main Street. Then she would go to meet them. Nina would hop off her pony, and the two girls – the one not quite as tall as the other, both of them slender – would walk to the barn on the school grounds, where they made sure the pony had plenty of mash and water for the rest of the day. When the three o'clock bell rang, they ran to the barn, cleaned and raked the stall, and then walked back to Mary's parents' house. They had their afternoon tea, practiced the piano, and did their homework until it was time for Nina to ride to her family's farm south of town to help with the chores.

* * * * * * * *

The first quarter of the new century had passed quickly, as time tends to do when there is work to be done. The girls sometimes wondered what would happen during the next 25 years, but they could only guess at what the future would bring.

More big buildings were built in Rushmore, including a hotel with a mansard roof. The townspeople called it the hotel with the French roof. It was across the street from the bank building, where there was a huge hall on the second floor, complete with stage. Locals gathered there for community events and activities. Those attending had to brave the steep "killer" steps to get up there and back down again.

The bank, the hotel, the park with its bandstand, and the depot lumber yard framed the town's main intersection. Those buildings are gone now, but grandpa and grandma's house, a block east of the intersection, is still standing.

* * * * * * * *

Two miles south of town, a new bridge was built across a tributary of Little Rock Creek. Three new sets of farm buildings were built along that stretch of road, one for each of the three Renselaar girls. The buildings were painted white; the doors and windows were trimmed in colonial green. They made an impressive sight as one came down the hill from town, crossed the creek, and started up the slope to the south.

Nina inherited the second farm on the right side of the road and married Erland, a rancher from South Dakota. Ten years later they adopted a little girl, Marin. When this child arrived, their happiness was unfettered. Family and friends – the whole community – rejoiced with them. They had waited so long.

* * * * * * *

Six years later, the tragedy of this child's death upended the lives of Nina, Erland, and all who knew them. Even today there are no words to describe the grief that took its place at Nina and Erland's table. Marin's death left its mark on every member of the extended Renselaar family for the next three generations.

* * * * * * *

At the time of Marin's death, my parents had been on the waiting list at Children's Home Society (CHS) in St. Paul for almost five years. Those who have gone through the adoption process know what it's like. For a long time, no one mentioned adoption to Nina and Erland. But then they changed their minds. It was not easy for them, but they wanted to try again, even though they were no longer young, and their age was against them.

One day, after sitting with Nina for a long time, Mother drove home and wrote a letter to CHS, asking if she and Dad could give their place on the waiting list to Nina and Erland. Mother said that seeing the two of them so sorrowful was more than she could bear. She didn't want them to have to wait any longer. If she and Dad could expedite matters in some way, she felt they would be blessed for the rest of their lives.

As it turned out, the wait for both couples was shorter than they had anticipated. Later that same year two letters from St. Paul arrived at the Rushmore post office. One was for Nina and Erland, the other was for my parents. A few months after that, two little girls came to live in Nobles County. One became my sister, Marie, and the other, Beverly, who could have become my sister had she been placed in a different bassinet, went to live with Nina and Erland.

* * * * * * * *

In October, 2011, Mother passed away at the Ecumen home for seniors in Worthington. She had celebrated her 100th birthday the previous January. My daughter and granddaughter came from their house on the shore of the "shining big sea water"[*] (Lake Superior) for the funeral. Beverly sat on their left. My friend Jerry came from Minneapolis and sat to my right. Mother, the youngest of her family, had outlived her sisters. My sister Marie, with whom Beverly had shared organist duties at their church, had died in November, 1994. There was a lot of room left on the church bench.

---

* Henry Wadsworth Longfellow, *The Song of Hiawatha*

After the service, Beverly and I spoke with each other about the letter Mother had written. We had only recently learned of its existence.

Minnesota Historical Society

Children's Home Society, St. Paul, Minnesota

Black-rimmed Glasses

Josh

Mother and Dad, together with Sam and Effie, thought the world of Josh. He was our hired man, but he was like a brother to both my parents, and I called him Uncle Josh. He was a gentle man. I never heard him raise his voice. Mother said he was the poet in our family. Josh was almost the same age as Dad. Josh's mother had been unable to care for him, so Sam and Effie took him in when he was tiny and raised him with their own children.

When Sam and Effie retired and moved to Rushmore, Dad and Josh ran the farm together.[*] When Dad and Mother married, Josh stayed on at the farm with them – not an unusual arrangement back then – keeping the room that had been his for as long as he could remember. The years passed.

* * * * * * * *

One Sunday afternoon, Mother's Iowa relatives came to visit. They brought their unmarried daughter, Emma, with them. She was

---

* When Dad's brother John (not to be confused with Dad's Uncle John, his cousin John, Mother's Uncle John, and later, me) married Rose Smith, he moved from our farm to hers. It was on the other side of Ridge Road, in Summit Lake Township – three miles from us – and it had a name: Apple Hill.

the same age as Mother, and Mother's middle name was Emma. They were both school teachers. Emma lived with her parents. She had never met Josh. They were introduced to each other, and then everyone went to sit in the living room. There wasn't much in the way of conversation. Mother thought of setting up the card table, but it was Sunday, and she knew that their pastor, Reverend Schaafsma, and his wife sometimes visited parishioners on Sundays. The whole congregation knew that those two did not approve of card-playing. Once, when the pastor and his wife appeared at our door unexpectedly, Dad scooped up all the cards from the table and threw them in the cookstove firebox. When the pastor asked what he was doing, Dad said, "Oh, I thought it was the county game warden." Apparently, everyone knew what that meant because no one asked any more questions.

Josh and Emma did not say a word, not even when everyone moved to the dining room table for tea and sat closer together. When the afternoon finally drew to a close, and Mother's relatives had gone, Dad looked at her and said, "I think that went well."

A year later, Emma and Josh were married. Their wedding picture sat on my parents' bedroom dresser through all my growing-up years, and I remember it well. Emma wore her glasses; they had thin black rims and the lenses were round, about the size of 50-cent pieces.

After the wedding, Emma continued living with her parents, and Josh stayed with us. There was a lot to do that year. A whole new set of farm buildings had to be constructed on land Sam and Effie owned in the next section. And then, just when everything seemed ready for the newlyweds to move in, a tornado destroyed the new house. I can still hear Dad say to Mother whenever they talked about it, "You know, I told you the day the first house blew down that it was not a good sign." "I remember," is all Mother ever said in reply.

Another house was built, and after two years of living apart, the young couple could be together. Mother often spoke of them and never failed to mention how happy they were. When you saw one, you knew the other was not far away. Emma helped Josh in the barns and out in the fields, and he helped her in the house and in the kitchen garden. Both my parents said it was beautiful to witness their devotion to each other. I think it made my parents' marriage stronger and more loving.

Toward the end of the fifth year, Emma began spending less time helping outside because she was "in the family way." A few months later, the baby tried to be born, but it was too early, and both Emma and the tiny child died at home, in the new house. Grandma Elsing said, "Poor little tyke, it was so eager to see them."

It was a terrible time. Sam and Effie moved back from town to stay with Josh at the new place. The preacher came to call, but left, saying he could not bear it. Almost everyone else stayed away. Josh moved back into his old room in my parents' house. Not long after that, Mother miscarried, and things were even worse than before because the winter that year was not only bleak, but also very cold.

My parents and Josh kept to themselves. They stopped going to church and went to town on off-days, early in the morning, when it wasn't likely there would be many people out and about. There were things that needed to be done: two sets of buildings to maintain and a full complement of animals to care for at both farm places.

One summer Sunday, Dad announced that he was going to church. Mother said she would go, too. They invited Josh to go with them, but he said he preferred to stay behind. They accepted that.

In those days church services were held in the early afternoon, and when they were over, members of the congregation gathered under the cottonwood trees in what had once been a horse pasture and ate lunch together. For many of them, it was the only social event of the week. People enjoyed it. They stayed together until the sun began its slow descent, and, sooner or later, someone would stand up and say, "Well, I guess we'd best be getting on home now; those cows sure aren't going to milk themselves." The shared time was over. Everyone stood up and prepared to leave. The sermon had given them something to think about, and visiting with relatives and friends had been pleasant.

Dad and Mother started out for the farm, but when they got close to their corner, they saw that the cows were still in the pasture. They thought that was odd. They wondered why Josh had not taken them in for milking. They put the car in the garage and went into the house, thinking that Josh had perhaps stayed too long at his nap. The house was quiet, and Mother called, "Josh, we're home." There was no answer. Dad started up the steps to Josh's room, slowly at first and then taking them two at a time. Nothing. He turned around. Mother was waiting at the foot of the stairs. Dad said, "Josh is not here."

"Well," Mother said, "maybe he's gone to the barn to get ready for the milking."

"Yes, you're probably right," Dad said, "that must be it; he's getting things ready for the milking. That must be what's happened."

Dad went to the barn, not bothering to change from his Sunday clothes. Mother followed him, still wearing her shiny black shoes. They entered the barn together and called for Josh again, but there was no answer there, either.

Then Dad turned around and began to run. He jumped over the lower part of the Dutch door and kept right on going. Alarmed by this, Mother followed after him as best she could. He ran across the yard, passed between the house and the milkhouse, and sprinted into the orchard, but first he shouted back to Mother, "Bring the car." Mum veered off to her right, toward the garage, and saw Dad just as he jumped the stile, heading for the old footbridge over the creek. He crossed it and disappeared into the small grove of willow saplings that marked the halfway point between Josh's house and ours. As Mother pulled out of our driveway and onto the road, she saw him starting up the lane to Josh's farmyard. When she reached it, she saw Dad go into the barn. At first she was surprised by that, but then, almost immediately, she knew. She stopped the car, left the motor running, and followed him. She opened the barn door and saw Dad's feet step off the haymow ladder and disappear into the loft. A heart-rending wail stopped her in her tracks.

"Josh," Dad cried, "No!"

Mother accustomed herself to the semi-darkness, climbed up into the hayloft, looked around and saw Dad tearing at the hayfork rope with his jackknife. The rope began to fray, then snapped, and a body fell to the hay-covered floor.

My parents reached Josh at the same time. His body was limp, his face an awful color. Mother looked at Dad and asked, "Is he dead?" Dad answered, "I don't know," and collapsed.

* * * * * * *

Josh survived, but he was fragile. The bond between him and my parents grew even stronger, and it lasted for as long as they lived.

Farm Footbridge

Malvolio, *Twelfth Night*, by William Shakespeare

Fig Éclairs

Neither my sister Marie nor I liked visiting Burt and Pearl. Mother and Dad had to work hard to get us to go there. First, they tried to cajole us. That never worked very well, so they usually moved on to outright bribery rather quickly. We could tell how difficult the struggle was going to be by how vague the bribes were. We held our ground until they turned into promises that were easy to remember and resulted in tangible things; however, we had learned not to push our luck. Our parents had better things to do than play mind games with us, and when it came to Burt and Pearl, we knew they could always fall back on the use of a secret weapon.

This weapon was not truly a secret, but it was powerful. We knew that, depending on the vagaries of their mood, our parents could deploy it in an instant if we crossed an invisible line into what they considered to be truculence, intransigence, or sheer obstinacy. We were always careful to follow the eddying rules as well as we could. Our parents were indulgent, and we enjoyed these little tugs of war, but there were limits.

They waited to see how bitterly we complained about the only treats Pearl ever had on offer: fig éclairs. Of all the awful things we were presented with as children, they were the worst.

Fig éclairs today are a far cry from what they used to be. None of them would ever recognize their desiccated ancestors from the days of yore if, by way of a wrinkle in time, they happened to meet up with them in a cupboard somewhere. Dry as a bone does not begin to convey any idea of what they were like. Little Sister said they were so hard and dry that one could scrape paint off large buildings with them.

If our parents allowed the discussion to get this far, we knew we were winning, but both Mother and Dad were canny opponents, and we never took anything for granted. We knew who called the shots. As far as our parents were concerned, privileges and other good things were invented so they could be withdrawn whenever it was deemed necessary. Mother and Dad were never pushovers, and the words "toss-up" and "draw" were not part of their vocabulary. None of us believed in halfway measures, compromises, or anything remotely resembling them. With us it was always down to the mat, and we all knew the quickest road to the mat was the one that led across the rickety bridge with the rusty iron girders and railings that transported only the most courageous across the Kanaranzi Creek chasm without causing heart palpitations. When our parents wanted to avoid long, drawn-out negotiations with us, all they had to do was invoke the spectral secret weapon – the spooky bridge at the bottom of the always-slippery hill road – and we could be drummed into submission.

On the night we're talking about here, Sister and I decided

to capitulate if our parents promised to use the road with the new bridge, even though it would take us several miles out of the way. They promised.

Dad thanked us for not dragging things out and making a fuss. He followed that with "Time's a-fleeting," and we left for Burt and Pearl's without further ado. As soon as we arrived there, Sister and I made a bee-line for the sunroom, where Pearl kept her collection of sunglasses. The magazines in this room were not like any we had at home. That very evening we learned that some actor, whose name was not yet a household word with us, had been arrested in Los Angeles for some big word that was still beyond our understanding. We did not have time to look it up in the dictionary because we were exhausted, and we soon fell asleep on Pearl's matching palm tree sofas.

We missed nine o'clock coffee (water for children), as well as the fig éclairs. I have only a faint memory of Dad carrying me to the car when it was time to go home. I could have awakened myself completely but chose not to. I liked being carried, even though I was too old for that sort of thing, but our parents spoiled us. People pursed their lips, but Mother and Dad didn't seem to mind. I don't think they cared a fig about what other people thought and said.

Once in the car, I knew Dad would carry me all the way up to my room when we got home, but first I had to stay awake long enough to make certain the two of them did not trick us by taking the scary bridge route home. In truth, they were not the kind of people who made promises and then broke them, but it's best in cases like this to be on one's guard.

As soon as we were on the right road, I closed my eyes, but before that happened, Dad said something that made quite an impression on me. I don't know why, but it did.

"You know, Mary," he said, "when it comes right down to it, that Burt is kind of a queer duck." I do not remember what, if anything, Mother said in response.

The requisite number of weeks passed, and then, early one evening, Burt and Pearl telephoned to ask if we were at home, and would it be OK for them to come calling. Sister and I had nothing against this because we knew they would not bring their fig éclairs with them.

Mother hung up the phone and said, "Malvolio and Pearl are coming over to visit for a while."

Marie and I never understood why Mother called Burt "Malvolio," but she did, except when he was in the room. One day we asked Dad about it. He said he thought it had something to do with the yellow socks Burt always wore. We doubted this could have been the real reason and decided Dad was joking. Years later, while reading Shakespeare's *Twelfth Night*, we learned that he had given us a straight answer.

Burt and Pearl arrived, and the evening exchange began. I liked taking part in grown-up conversation, but on this particular night I couldn't think of anything to say. The time passed slowly until – all of a sudden – I remembered having something of my own to add. I was sure everyone would be interested in hearing what it was.

I went up to Burt. He was talking, but he had been talking for quite a while, and I didn't think he would mind my having a turn. I tapped him on the knee and said, "Burt, my daddy says . . . ," but Burt apparently did not hear me. At any rate, he took no notice. However, I saw that Dad had begun paying attention to me. That was encouraging, so I tapped Burt's knee again. Still no response. By now Mother, too, was leaning forward in her chair. I tried again, and this time I got through.

"Burt," I said, "my daddy says you're kind of a queer duck."

These few words gained the attention of everyone in the room, including some neighbors and the hired help who had stopped in for a while. In fact, it was now quite a large group, but they were all very quiet, including those who were sitting out on the porch.

Burt was silent for a moment. Then he looked at me and said, "Little man, if you were just a bit older, I would believe you."

* * * * * * * *

My father told this story until old age overtook him, and it always ended with the same words: that if Burt had only looked at Dad's face at that moment, he would have realized at once that the "little man" was not making this up.

Buckingham Palace, London

Ernie

Ernie's father died in an airplane crash at the Nobles County fairgrounds, and Ernie and his brother had to go fight in the South Pacific years before any of their cousins had to go to war to make the world safe for democracy again.

Ernie did not mind too much when his draft notice appeared in our mail box. It came to our house because Ernie had lived with us for a long time. He stayed in the north bedroom, the one at the top of the stairs, on the right. We called it the "ice box" because it was the coldest room in the house. It had no heat register in the floor, so no warmth from the stoves downstairs could get up there. Dad had slept in that room when he was a boy, and he told us it was so cold that water for washing one's face in the morning froze in the pitcher during the night. Whenever Sister and I complained about the cold, Dad told us we were lucky to have heat registers in our rooms and that we should be glad Queen Victoria was not our mother because she made all her children take cold showers every morning, summer and winter alike. He also said she lived in a shoe, but Mother showed us a picture of Buckingham Palace and said maybe the queen and her many children only lived in the shoe during the summer.

Our family left bedroom doors open in winter for Ernie's

sake. He said the "ice box" was the nicest room he had ever had, and that he would be sorry to leave it for a bunk in an army barracks.

Sister and I cried the day Ernie had to board the train that took him away to war. He said, "I'll be back before you can say 'Peas porridge hot, peas porridge cold, peas porridge in the pot nine days old,' " but we didn't think that was possible.

After breakfast that morning he took us out to the old garage, opened the big door, and led us inside. He showed us how to open the shutters and said if we missed him a lot while he was away, we could go in there any time we wanted to and sit with his car. He gave us the key for the side door of the garage and told us where he kept it. He locked the big door with a different key, put it in a red tin box, and hid it beneath the floorboards under the workbench.

His car was on blocks and covered by a tarp; the wheels were wrapped with gunny sacks. Ernie showed us the mouse cages. We knew how to use them and promised that if we ever caught a mouse in his garage, we would carry the cage somewhere far away before releasing the animal. The three of us sat at the workbench, and when it was time to leave, Sister and I took turns locking and unlocking the side door.

"This place is only for the two of you to visit," Ernie said. "I don't want you ever to bring anyone else in here, except for your parents, of course, if you wish. And no food. Do you understand?"

We nodded our heads to indicate we understood. Then we closed the shutters and left. Mother and Dad were waiting out front.

Ernie's bag was already in the trunk. We got in the car and drove away. Ernie looked back once. No one said anything. We all knew we were not going to see him again for a long time.

* * * * * * *

One day Mother changed the calendar to a new month and outlined one of the days near the bottom of the page with stick-on stars.

"Why are those stars green?" Marie asked.

"Because green is for hope," Mother said. "We hope the grass and the leaves on the trees will all come back in the spring."

"And they do," said Sister.

"Yes, they do," said Mother, "every year."

"Is it spring now?" I asked.

"Yes, it is," she answered.

"Will Ernie come back soon?" I continued.

"Yes, he will," Mother said. "He is coming home on this day," and she pointed to the day with the stars on it. "Today is the first day of the month. I'm going to X it out, and tomorrow morning we will X out the second day. When all the days between now and the starred day are crossed through, it will be time to fetch Ernie from the train station."

That was a long month for Marie and me. We were up early on the last day. It was Dad's turn to make the X, but he made a big star instead.

When we reached the station platform, there were not as many people as there had been on the day when Ernie and the other soldiers left.

"Aren't their families coming to meet them?" Sister asked. "Won't they be happy to see them again?"

"Some of the soldiers who left with Ernie won't be coming back today," Mother said.

"Will they be arriving on a later train?" I asked.

"Yes," Dad answered.

"Can we wait for them?" I went on.

"No," he said.

"Why not?" I asked.

"Because they are coming in on a funeral train, and their return will be private," he answered. "The people who work here will cordon off the station with black drapery, and we will be asked to leave. The only people allowed to stay will be family members of the young men who were killed in action. They will be coming back in wooden coffins draped in black. Everything will be black, except for the flags. The families will be wearing black and so will the people who work for the railroad. Even the flowers will be black because the loss of a soldier, sailor, or airman is a sad thing. Using black is a way to show we care and respect the grief that those families who have lost loved ones are suffering. They will all go out to the cemetery in the black cars you see over there on the other side of the railroad tracks," and he pointed in that direction.

Ernie's train was late, and we had to wait a long time. There was a band, but it didn't play. We asked why not. The lady standing next to us said it was because the funeral train was coming in soon after the passenger train. There would be no music until the people in our group had gone home, and the passenger train had gone on to the next town. When the funeral train and the grieving families were all alone, the band would play sad music called a dirge.

* * * * * * * *

We saw Ernie right away. His window was open, and he and his buddies were leaning out of it. The train wasn't going very fast, and we were able to walk right up to it. People were crying. We cried, too, even Dad, who did not cry often.

After the train stopped, Ernie reached for Marie and held her in mid-air for a while. I was too big for that. Dad handed Marie to Mother, then he lifted me up, and Ernie put his arms around my shoulders.

Ernie got off the train, and we stayed together for a while in the shade of the depot roof. He took off his cap and gave it to me to hold. We were all surprised to see how short his hair was, and he was surprised to see how much Little Sister and I had grown.

When we arrived home, cousin Mil – mother's helper – took pictures of us. Ernie had told us in a letter that he had lost weight, so none of us said anything about it, but as Mil was taking pictures, Mother's eyes filled with tears. Maybe she was afraid that the suit we had ordered for him would be too big. We all helped Ernie take his bags up to his room, and he said it was good to be home. We were happy to have him back.

Sister and I went downstairs, and Ernie joined us a little while later for tea. After that he went out to see his car, and we walked through the new rows of shelter-belt trees to show him how much they had grown since we had planted them together. Mother and Mil made some of Ernie's favorite things for our light supper that evening, but I cannot recall what they were. It had been a big day for us. After Sister and I were dressed for bed, we went downstairs to say goodnight to everyone, but especially to Ernie. He held us on his knees, and Mother took more pictures. Dad took us upstairs to bed. We said our prayers. When we came to the line, "If I should die before I wake," I remembered the black at the depot.

* * * * * * * *

It didn't happen the first night Ernie was home, but later that week I woke up in the middle of the night. Someone was crying softly. I crept out of bed, put on my slippers, and tip-toed down the hall to Ernie's room. His door was open. I went in, stood at the side of his bed, and waited. The crying turned to sobbing. Ernie sat up and hugged his knees. I touched his hand and said, "Ernie, Ernie, wake up."

He woke up, looked at me and said, "Hi there, little John." Then he patted the top of my head, turned over, and went back to sleep.

The next morning I told my parents that Ernie had cried during the night, and that I had gone in and awakened him. They told me not to do that again because it might frighten him.

The dreams continued as Ernie got older. He took pills to help him sleep, but the dreams never went away completely. They stayed with him for the rest of his life. Ernie has been dead a long time now, but sometimes when I'm awake at night, I think I hear him crying.

Courtesy Janet Larson and Lester Boots

Ernie

The Milkmaid, Johannes Vermeer, 1632-1675

Loss

Rory was his name, and I only met him once. Aunt Clara had invited several families, including his, to a party at her club. It was raining when we arrived, so guests wandered through the public rooms and looked at the paintings on the walls.

Whenever Sister and I were taken to museums or art galleries, we passed the time by taking notes and then choosing our three favorite paintings. When we finished looking around, we checked with each other to see if we had chosen some of the same things. We hadn't finished making our choices when we were called to the dining room for lunch. Dad helped Marie find her place card, and I found mine by myself. Mother was not with us; she was being treated for pleurisy at the Adrian hospital.

We stood behind our chairs and waited for Aunt Clara to lead us in the table grace song. Auntie was a shy person; when she spoke, her eyes were half-closed most of the time. However, she was the most musical person in Mother's family and always led the singing at gatherings like this one. She did not close her eyes when she sang. After grace, there was a general shuffling of chairs, and we sat down.

Most of those present knew one another, so there weren't many introductions, but I had to say my name to the person on my right, and he told me his name was Rory. His family had only recently moved into the house next to Aunt Clara's. Rory saw my notes on the table and asked about them. I explained the game Sister and I had been playing and added that we hadn't had enough time to choose three, so that's why there were only two. The first was a Native American sitting on his horse. The horse and rider looked sad and dejected. Rory asked how did I know it was a Native American? I answered, "Because he had feathers in the band that crossed his forehead."

I asked Rory if he had a favorite painting. He said he liked the one that showed a country road lined with tall, skinny trees. The branches were all bunched near the tops of the trees. Rory said the painter's name was Hobbema, and he thought that was a Dutch name.

"Yes," I said, "I remember that painting."

Rory talked with me throughout the meal. That was nice. Usually at events like this one, I had no one to talk to. My maternal cousins, with one exception, were all older, in high school or beyond, and they didn't seem to have much to say to someone my age. Rory told me he was a junior in high school, and I said I was still in elementary school, but I think he knew that already.

After lunch there was a slide show presentation. Cousin Matthew was an officer in the Air Force on furlough from Charleston Air Force Base in South Carolina. He had a new camera that he'd bought at the PX.

I could not see over the heads of people sitting in front of us, so Rory held me on his knees. That was better. The sun had come out by the time the program was over, and we all moved out to the terrace. My family and I were still dressed for church, but I asked Dad if I could go wading in the children's pool, and he nodded his agreement. I left my shoes and socks at Rory's table and walked over to the water.

At first I just sat on the edge, dangling my feet in the water and splashing around a bit. Then I stood up, took one step in the water, and fell down. I had stepped on something sharp and I heard glass break. I tried to go back to where I'd been sitting, but children and some adults began screaming. I turned around and saw a trail of blood in the water. I fell down again, and when I woke up, Rory was holding me, asking if I was all right. He was wearing his tennis whites, and his shirt was more red than white. His trousers and even his shoes were bloody. Dad held my hands, and he was getting bloody, too.

Aunt Clara came running around the corner of the cabana line. She looked as if she'd seen a ghost. I knew at that moment that she loved me very much, and I knew why.

Very gently she wrapped cloth napkins around the ball of my foot. Only a piece of skin connected it to the rest of me. I was frightened. Club personnel brought white towels and began mopping up blood that seemed to be everywhere. An ambulance arrived and drove right across the tennis courts to pick me up. Rory carried me inside and held me on his lap. Dad looked in and said he would follow in our car. Rory said that would be fine. He stayed with me right into the emergency room. Dad joined us there, and the three of us watched as the ball of my foot was sewn back in place.

* * * * * * * *

That was the last time I saw Rory. A year later he was in the hospital, and Mother told me he had died. Rheumatic fever had weakened his heart. There were no antibiotics to help him in those days. I began to cry. Dad took me in his arms. I noticed that Mother was wearing hospital slippers. Dad said, "Your mother has come home from the hospital just for today to be with you because she knows Rory was your best friend. You talked about him so often. Try to be strong for her."

I sat up straight. Dad told me Mother was too weak for a hug, and that I should just hold her hand a little. She touched my hand, and then a nurse wheeled her away. Cousin Mil came in and hugged me. I cried for a long time. I was hurting a lot, but I didn't know at that time there was a word to describe those feelings.

Rory

JAMES I
1603-1625

Portrait of King James

King James
(1566 – 1625)

History sometimes moves in mysterious ways. James, the son of Mary Stuart, Queen of Scots, was also the heir of Elizabeth Tudor, Queen of England, and is known as both James I and James VI. Elizabeth and Mary were cousins. For more than four hundred years, James has been remembered as the man who gave his name to the King James Version of the Bible.

Unanswered Question

I.   Gramma Hardy

Gramma Hardy wore her hair in a bun, walked with a Bryn Mawr stride, and drove her own car. Except for the bun, she was everything most grandmothers are not. She was not demure, or petite, and most of all, she was not a homebody. Also, she was not really our grandmother. We just called her that. She was the town's "go to" person. Everyone knew that if you wanted something done – and done well – the first thing you did was speak with her.

She lived across the street from the "English" church in Rushmore. Some people said God lived across the street from her. Long after Gramma's death, I gave Mother a book called *God's Secretaries, The Making of the King James Bible,* written by Adam Nicolson. Mother took one look at the title and said, "You know, that's what Gramma Hardy was, God's secretary."

Gramma was a vibrant force in the life of our family during the years when it seemed that Mother spent more time in the Adrian hospital with pleurisy than she did at home with us. I asked Dad, "Why can't pleurisy come out to the farm and spend some time with us, rather than Mother always having to go into town to spend time with her?"

Sister and I missed having Mother at home, and Dad wasn't there much either because he spent most of his free time at the hospital. One of Mother's nieces looked after us. We liked Mil a lot, but she had rules, and neither Sister nor I liked rules. Marie did not like having to take naps in the afternoon, and I didn't like having to make my bed in the morning, but Mil was vigilant. We didn't escape our chores very often, but we kept trying. Mil told her mother we were spoiled. Aunt Jennie went on with her work.

Rob was Mil's boyfriend. One evening when he came to pick her up for a date, Sister and I made such a fuss about her leaving that they took us along with them. The next day we told Dad they had bought us ice cream sodas at the local drug store, but Dad never allowed us to go on another date with them.

* * * * * * * *

Whenever Gramma Hardy came to visit, we jumped up and down and ran out to meet her at the front gate because we knew Mil's rules would not be enforced until Gramma drove away. Sometimes Gramma took us with her to the hospital where Mother was. Gramma felt sorry for us. Once I heard her refer to us as *pauvres petits enfants*. I asked Mil what that was, and she said, "It's French for kids, just like you."

In those days children were not permitted to visit patients

in hospitals, not even if the patient was your mother whom you had not seen for a long time. However, Gramma had ways of getting around rules. She called it "circumventing." She would settle us in the waiting room and go up the stairway to the landing. She stopped there, waved to us, and then continued up the stairs.

Sometimes, if there wasn't too much activity in the halls, she would return to where we were, put on her long black coat and say, "Come on, we're going circumventing." To me it was as exciting as going on an elephant hunt. She wrapped her big coat around us, and we all went up the stairs to the landing. When we got there, we stopped, raised our hands to our foreheads, and scanned the horizon for elephants.

On the landing there were several blue and white urns filled with ferns whose fronds were almost as large as palm tree branches. They reminded me of pictures in Rudyard Kipling's jungle stories. Gramma parted the fronds, and we pushed our way through them to the wicker chairs and divan over by the windows. They were positioned to give the people who sat in them a view of the high school athletic field. Gramma sat in the middle. She wrapped one big sleeve around Sister and the other one around me. None of us said a word.

When the coast was clear, we made our way through the ferns again, walked up the stairs to the next floor and down the hall into Mother's room. We waited at the door, waved to her, and she waved back. We were quiet, and we didn't stay long. Gramma slipped off her coat, went to kiss Mother on the cheek, returned, wrapped us in the coat again, and we left.

* * * * * * * *

On the way out of town, we stopped at the bakery to buy pastry for teatime at home with Mil. When Gramma visited us, Sister and I did not have to help Mil clear the tea things from the table, as we did when we were alone with Dad.

After tea we ran to look at the books Gramma had brought with her. She always had books for us. Sometimes they were new, but more often they were not. I remember some of the titles: *Black Beauty*, *King of the Hills*, *Alice in Wonderland*, *Lassie Come Home*, and – best of all – Robert Louis Stevenson's *A Child's Garden of Verses* with its thick cover and colored pictures. While visiting Edinburgh, Scotland, with my family in 2017, I looked for a book like this one, but failed to find it.

Whenever Gramma gave us a book, she said, "This is your book to read for a while, but not to keep forever."

One day I saw the name "Dirk" written in the Tom Sawyer book. It was a schoolboy's handwriting, not much different from my own, and I wondered who that was. I asked myself if all the books Gramma gave us would one day go back to him, but as the years went by, I noticed that none of the books she gave us were ever taken away.

II.   Kissed by an Angel

Two of the most beautiful things in our house seemed not to belong there. Sister and I were always intrigued by them. The first reminded us of Little Red Riding Hood's world. It was a shoulder wrap, but it came from a silver fox, not from a wolf. It was kept in a big kind of hat box on the top shelf of an upstairs closet across the hall from Marie's room. Sometimes she modeled it for us. It trailed along behind her, and Mother would ask her to be careful. This wrap had a lining with snaps on it, so it could be attached to a long coat. I do not know where it came from, but it was always clear to me that our parents did not buy it.

Mother had another stole, made from mink that Dad caught on his trap line,[*] but Sister and I preferred the silver fox because it was so soft. Marie said it was probably magical. It looked as if there were dozens of thin silver threads running through the grey-black fur, and we often brushed it lightly against our faces. It was like being kissed by an angel.

The second item was a purse. It was longer and slightly wider than a leather glove. Inside it there was room enough for a tissue, not much more. The purse was made of a shiny metallic material by the Whiting and Davis Company in the 1920s, and it glittered. It had a soft lining and was kept in a velvet-lined drawer in a small chest next

---

[*] Uncle John's antique trap collection is at the Minnesota Historical Society in St. Paul.

to Mother's dressing table in the downstairs bedroom. This table had a matching mirror where she could sit and look at herself, but we never saw her do that. On the dressing table there was a framed photo in sepia tones of Mother and her sister Lillie seen in profile, both of them looking off to the left.

There were built-in closets in the hall between the downstairs bedroom and the dining room. Mother's coats and hats were kept there. One of the closet doors had a full-length mirror, and she always stopped in front of it to check her hemline when she put on a coat and prepared to leave the house.

* * * * * * * *

Sister and I almost never went into the downstairs bedroom. It was used mostly when Mother was at home between bouts of pleurisy, and I remember staying in that room when I had the mumps and the measles. When Sister had scarlet fever, she had to stay in that room for a long time. At night Mother and Dad took turns sleeping in the room next to it. They always left the connecting door open because Marie was afraid of being alone. The house was under quarantine when she had scarlet fever. "Doc" Waller nailed a warning sign to the kitchen door. The weeks went by, and then one day he came out to the farm in his LaSalle car, took the sign down, and burned it on the retaining wall between the kitchen extension and the new garage.

* * * * * * * *

When we were in high school, Sister and I were invited to a party where the guests were asked to dress like people dancing the Charleston in the 1920s. When we told Mother about the party, she went into the downstairs bedroom and returned with the 1920s purse. We had seen it before, but not often. Sister asked if she could take it to the dance, but Mother wasn't keen on that idea. Instead, she and Dad played our Charleston record and showed us how to do the crossing hands and knees part. Mother and Dad were both good dancers and always said they were glad we lived near the Catholic town of Wilmont because they had lots of dances there.

Courtesy Ribnick Luxury Outerwear, Minneapolis

Silver Fox Fur

Alice's Adventures in Wonderland

III.   I'll Tell You No Lies

Like most children, Marie and I had lots of questions for our parents. Like most parents, Mother and Dad answered these questions in various ways. Sometimes they chose not to answer us at all. When that happened, we knew better than to pester them by repeating the question. We were raised to understand that "No means no."

But there was a gray area between a straight answer and no answer at all. In the years before we went to school, if our parents said, "Children should be seen and not heard," it meant some leeway was allowed, and we could continue the conversation.

During the fantastical grade school years, Mother turned to *Alice in Wonderland* and said we should take care when asking questions lest we "fall down the rabbit hole." This could mean almost anything. There was also an air of danger about it because no one had much idea of what life was like in a rabbit hole.

By the time we were in high school, the admonition had grown darker: "Ask me no questions, and I'll tell you no lies." This had an edge to it. It meant there are secrets in this world, and it's best to stay away from them. End of discussion.

In college, and continuing into adulthood, Mother and Dad parried our questions with "Never apologize, never explain." This was sometimes followed by "What's your business is your business – no one else's – and it's best to keep it that way." By now Sister and

I had some secrets of our own, so we decided the best thing for all concerned was simply to respect one another's privacy. For a long time that worked very well.

* * * * * * * *

One day not long after Mother celebrated her one-hundredth birthday, I asked her a question I had thought about from time to time for many years. Before answering, she looked at me without surprise and said, "For now we see through a glass darkly, but then we shall see face to face."[*]

I repeated the question, "Who was Dirk?"

"Oh, you know who that was," she said. "He was Gramma's son."

I had the feeling she had rehearsed everything, and now it was up to me to connect the dots.

---

[*] 1 Corinthians 13:12

Ferns

Calhoun Beach Club apartment photos, Minneapolis

Camelback Sofa

I was in second grade when I walked up to my piano teacher's house for the first time and rang the bell. She came to the door and invited me in. The living and dining rooms had been combined into one large rectangular space. She pointed to a camelback sofa on the window side of that room and said I could wait there. I climbed up on the sofa and made myself comfortable. My feet did not quite touch the floor.

"As soon as I finish with the pupil at the piano, it will be your turn," she said. "Do you mind waiting?"

"No," I answered.

She went to the piano, seated herself on a café chair next to it, and the lesson continued.

A black cocker spaniel trotted out of the kitchen, came across to the sofa, and jumped up next to me. We had hunting dogs and a collie at home, but this was the first time I'd had a chance to pet a spaniel. Almost at once I knew that visiting this house for my weekly lesson would be fun.

To those who knew my teacher as the banker's wife, she was Mrs. D. C. Shore. To most people in the town, she was Mrs. Del Shore. Her friends called her Dorothy. To her pupils, she was Mrs.

Shore. She became an important part of my life, not just because she was my piano teacher, but because of the way she viewed the world. Although she lived in a small town, she was not small-minded. She was part of a larger community, one she shared with all those for whom a love of music is as natural as breathing in and out.

Music helped define who she was, and I wanted to be like that. She was someone for me to admire and try to emulate. Chopin and his nocturnes, Schubert and his songs, Haydn and his sonatas were all second nature to her, and I hoped one day they would be that for me, too. Mrs. Shore was a real and sustaining presence in my life. Years later, she was somehow there beside me at Franz Schubert's birthplace in Vienna and when I visited Francis Poulenc's small château on the Loire River near the ancient city of Tours, in France.

* * * * * * * *

Parents should take care when choosing the people who will have significant roles in the lives of their children. By teaching me to play music as the composers themselves had played it, Mrs. Shore made it come alive and for that I will always be grateful. To this day I regard those composers as my great good friends, and I think she felt that way, too.

The joy of music – to be able to sit down and play something that was first captured on paper two hundred years ago or more – helps establish a connection that is both meaningful and miraculous.

It is a simple gift, within the reach of all of us, but it's a lesson most of us never would have learned without the tutelage of someone who was willing to take the time to pass along to us what others had shared with them.

I no longer have a piano of my own, but there is one nearby, and two small camelback sofas sit facing each other in my living room. They brighten my life, and I often think of Mrs. Shore and her black spaniel when I look at them.

Mrs. Shore recognized my rambunctiousness and channeled it. She included Liszt and Rachmaninoff among the pieces she chose for me to play in recital, but I sensed a difference when she switched me to a Chopin Polonaise. She prepared me for Johann Sebastian Bach, whose music I would one day sing with Dr. Arnold Running's Augustana College choir. I always liked Bach's chorales because they had lots of notes, and I enjoyed learning all the parts: soprano, alto, tenor, and bass.

Today, looking back, I remember Mrs. Shore's restraint most of all. I had been taking piano lessons from her for several years when friends of our family came from California to visit. The woman was also a piano teacher, and she asked me to play something for her. I sat down and played a short piece. When it was over, the visitor said, "You can make that more interesting by playing octaves with your left hand." I thought that was a good idea and repeated the piece with as many octaves as I could find. Then she said I could play chords rather than just one or two notes with the left hand. I tried that, too, until I was able to play a lot louder. After the Californians left, I went through my music and added notes all over the place.

At my next lesson, I asked Mrs. Shore if she would like to hear me play the new things I had learned.

"Yes," she said, so I sat down and began. All these additional notes seemed to work best in a short piece by Mozart. I played it twice because it was just a short piece. Mrs. Shore sat to my right, as she always did, and listened.

When it was over, I looked at her, expecting her approval. She did not really disapprove, but seemed to consider carefully what she had just heard. Then she looked at me, smiled, and said, "Thank you for playing that for me. It was nice, but how about we just continue playing it the way Mozart wrote it?"

From then on, that's what I did.

Wolfgang Amadeus Mozart (1756-1791)

High Clipped Hedge

Long, long thoughts

As Mother and I drove down the lane past the machine shop, our hired man, Ray, called out and said, "Mary, Herman says to leave the boy in town with Sam and Effie in case you have to drive all the way to Sioux Falls. That's too long a trip for him."

Mum dropped me off in our small town to spend the afternoon with Dad's parents while she drove on to a larger place that had a John Deere dealership. Dad needed a spare part in case the combine broke down again.

Spending time with my grandparents was always special. They told me stories about Holland, the "old country," and I read aloud for them. We had good times together. I carried a book or two with me wherever I went because it sometimes happened that I was left alone with nothing to do for long periods of time while Dad helped blacksmiths at their forges, carpenters in lumber yards, or dusty people high up in grain elevators where it was too dangerous for a little boy like me to follow. Sometimes my days were long and solitary, but time with Sam and Effie always passed quickly.

Before tea in the afternoon, Sam and I weeded the flower beds. He told me it was a waste of precious time not to get all of the roots out of the ground, worse actually than not weeding at all. When we finished, we went indoors for tea. While we had our afternoon break, Dad's parents talked about the Netherlands. When that was over, they asked me to read for them.

In good weather we sat in the garden. They moved the slatted benches so we could sit in the shade of the high hedge that ran the length of the driveway, all the way from the street to the one-car garage in back of the house. Sam and Effie sat on one bench, and I had the other. No one spoke. I showed them my book and began reading the story about the Dutch boy who saved his town by plugging a small hole in a dike when he noticed water trickling out from its base. I remember telling my grandparents the boy was brave to stay out at the dike alone when it was getting dark. Neither of them said anything, and I wondered if I had been too talkative for them. They never interrupted me when I was reading, and I liked that about them. Even when I was small, I did not like interruptions when people were reading aloud. Sam and Effie always waited for me to finish, and then they asked their questions, but this day was different. They asked me no questions. They were quieter than usual, and that means really, really quiet because they were quiet to begin with. Even though I did not quite know the meaning of the word "solemn" at that time, I realized later that it described them. It was as if they were remembering things from times gone by. I had the feeling we were sitting out at the dike – in silence – waiting, just the three of us.

Dutch Dike

Heartland Cook Stove

Grace

Relatives had recently had a furnace installed, a huge black monster of a thing with air ducts as big around as five-gallon pails that spread out across the basement ceiling and up into all parts of the house. It looked like a grotesque black spider that had escaped from a horror movie. None of our other country cousins had furnaces in their houses, so this hulk was an object of interest. All of us went down to the basement to look at it, and that's when the trouble started.

In the 1940s, before these cousins were in high school, our families celebrated birthdays together. For Sister and me, these were not happy occasions. When we saw our cousins one family at a time, things went well enough, but when two or more families visited, the cousins ganged up on us, and that is what they were doing now.

A cousin who lived in the house took a deck of cards with her, opened the door to the furnace room, and went inside. The other cousins dragged card tables and chairs sufficient for all of them into the new space. Then they closed and locked the door behind them, thus preventing Sister and me from entering. More than once I tried to open the door, but it wouldn't budge. Certain that it was unfair of them to lock us out, I knocked on the door several times and asked them to open up. No answer, but we could hear them talking and laughing in there. After making further objections, Marie and I went upstairs and told our aunts that their children were not playing with us. It occurred to me that my aunts might ask who in the world would want to go into that furnace room anyway. The furnace was coal-fired, so the room was bound to be dirty and dusty, and they knew I didn't like dust. But I wanted to go in there, dusty or not, and thought I had a right to do so.

Aunt Gwendolyn turned to her sister and said, "Oh, Herman's children always have something to grouse about." This was news to me. She made no attempt to prevent me from hearing what she said. I decided this was insulting, and it wasn't the first time Sister and I had been on the receiving end of this kind of behavior. We already knew that our cousins didn't think the two of us were worth their time or trouble.

Dad was not with us that day. He was visiting Mother in the hospital. He spent a lot of time there, and we knew he would not return for us until late afternoon. It looked to me as if it would be a long day with nothing much for us to do. Things like this had happened before, but this time I decided to take action. I took Marie's hand, and we left the room where our uncles and aunts were sitting. They watched us go.

We went out to the mud room and down the half-flight of stairs to the landing. I pulled our coats off the hooks. We sat down on the steps, put on our overshoes, and buckled them. It was not easy. Even though I had read sixty library books that year, and my picture had been in an Iowa newspaper, I had not yet learned how to tell my left foot from my right. There had always been someone available to help with shoes and boots. When we finished that job, we put on our coats, scarves, caps and mittens. Then we got up, opened the double doors, and left the house. It was cold outside, above freezing, but not by much. We walked out of the cottonwood grove and down the driveway onto the township road.

"Where are we going?" Sister asked.

"Home," I answered.

She looked at me in wonder and asked in a voice that children sometimes employ when faced with situations that are beyond their comprehension, "Isn't that kind of far?"

"It's a mile," I said, although I thought it was farther than that. She took my hand, and we started out.

It was a long way home, but we made it. As we came down the hill and reached the line of trees that bordered what had once been the sheepfold, we passed the tenant house. The hired man's wife, Llewellyn, ran to meet us. She took us into her house because it was closer than our house up on the circle. We sat down in front of the cookstove.

Llewellyn did not ask what we were doing out in the cold on a day like this. She warmed our hands in hers, and then she checked to see if we had any white frozen patches on our cheeks. She heated milk for us and served it with honey. There was no telephone in her house at that time, so she could not call anyone to ask what was going on. Later we learned that our aunts told Dad we had gone out to the barn to play, and that's why no one came looking for us until he returned from the hospital late that afternoon to pick us up.

Llewellyn walked with us through the front pasture to our own house, where Mil gave us raspberry jam on toast to eat. Then we got ready for bed. Sister fell asleep as she was being carried up the stairs. By the time Dad arrived home, I was also fast asleep. He did not awaken us.

I was up early the next morning, dressed myself, and went down to the kitchen. Breakfast was on the table. Mil said, "Good morning," and sat down with me. We started eating. I wondered why we did not wait for the rest of the family, but I was hungry and did not ask any questions. A few minutes later Dad came in from outside. He washed his hands, sat down, and began eating his poached egg. Sister struggled in, dragging both her Teddy bears. She was hungry, but she climbed up on her chair and waited. A minute passed, then she looked up at Dad and asked, "Aren't we going to say grace?"

Dad looked back at her, touched her chin, and said, "Grace is over."

Father Helping Son with Overshoes

Connor and Nora

Corn Picking

I.   Horses

When I went to live at the farm in the late 1930s, there were no tractors, and when I left for college almost twenty years later, there were no workhorses. Times had changed.

Connor and Nora were our last two workhorses. Dad always said they were the best team he had ever had. We found a good home for Connor, and Nora stayed with us a while longer. She had gone lame, and Dad wanted her last days to be spent in familiar surroundings.

When the horse trailer arrived on the yard, Dad and I walked to the barn and brought both horses out to the loading dock. Connor got in first. Nora wanted to follow, but we held her back. Connor balked when he realized Nora wasn't going with him. Mother came out of the house when she heard the whinnying. She said it was one of the saddest moments of her life.

Connor backed out of the trailer, and Nora went over to nuzzle against him. He returned this greeting, as horses do. Dad walked the two of them around the windmill circle, and Connor calmed down.

When they got near the trailer, Connor tossed his head a

few more times, then he stood shoulder to shoulder with Nora for a minute. When Dad took hold of his halter, Connor followed him up the ramp and into the trailer. Nora turned away, limped back to the barn and into her stall without urging from any of us.

I heard Dad say, "We should call the vet," but Mother said, "Let's wait a few more days."

A month later we buried Nora in the horse pasture west of the old vegetable garden. When Mother and I restored the garden in the late 1990s, we found traces of Nora's burial place not far from where Sam's avenue of cottonwood trees had been.

After the burial, Dad said, "Come on, we'll take the tractor over to Louie and Minnie's. I want to look at that new corn picker they've got." Louie was the first in our community to stop picking corn by hand. We were the next.

II.   Machinery

A corn picker is a machine that has teeth and claws. It tears the ears of corn off the stalks and removes the husks. Unlike dragons, corn pickers do not spit fire, but they rattle and shake like the wild things in Maurice Sendak's famous book for children. They are infernal machines that can strike fear in the hearts of the timid, and even the not-so-timid. In the 1940s they got their power from the tractors that pulled them through the fields. Today's corn pickers are self-propelled.

The corn-picking season is short, and time is of the essence. Some farmers pick corn around the clock. People driving along Interstate 90 in southern Minnesota at night sometimes stop at the Perkins restaurant in Worthington and ask, "What are those spooky lights out there in the fields?"

In the late 1990s, when I went out to the field at night to wait for the corn picker to come up to the end of the row, its lights reminded me of the glowing eyes of Fafner in the guise of a dragon in Richard Wagner's opera, *Siegfried*. When I mentioned this to Mother, she smiled and said I had a good imagination.

Life on the nation's farms was transformed when machines appeared in the fields. Gone were the days when farmers and their families walked beside their horse-drawn wagons picking corn by hand for hours at a time, day after day. Breaking the ears off the stalks and tearing away the husks was hard work, but if you were lucky, you developed a technique that made it a little easier. Hearing the plunk of each ear as it hit the wagon's sideboards helped pass the time. It also helped if you had someone to talk to, but it was always hard work, and there wasn't a lot of talking back and forth. Dad said he imagined the ears of corn hitting the wagon as pieces of gold dropping into his coffer at the bank. Mother said he also had a good imagination.

Working with corn-picking machines was dangerous. They were unforgiving. Many farmers paid a heavy price for a moment of carelessness. It took valuable time to shut down a machine. Those who operated them sometimes grew impatient, forgot themselves, and ended up tempting fate.

Sometimes clumps of earth were torn up with the stalks and jammed the rollers. A farmer who sought to dislodge the clumps by trying to kick them through did so at his peril; he risked being pulled into the jaws of the monster machine.

A few years after Dad and I went to look at Louie's new corn picker, Louie got caught in it. A torn pant leg became entangled in the whirling machinery and quickly pulled him down.

By the late 1940s it was rare to find a country preacher who could look out at his congregation on a Sunday morning and not see a farmer sitting there who had, at some point, been caught in a corn picker and now walked with a bad limp or a cane. Some farmers lost an arm or a leg; others lost their lives.

III.   Louie & Minnie

Minnie was going about her work up on the farmyard. She could hear the tractor and picker going up and down the corn rows out in the field nearest the house. There was a rhythm to the sound; it was loudest when Louie turned the rig around at the end of a row near the farm buildings. After that, the sound gradually diminished as he drove over the crest of the ridge and down to the far end of the field, where he turned around again. The noise grew louder as he made his way back up to Ridge Road.

Minnie was working in her garden when she first became aware that something had changed. The rhythm had broken. Louie should have been back to her end of the field by now, but he wasn't. Now and then there was a breakdown, and she wondered if that's what had happened, but quickly dismissed that idea. If he had had a breakdown, he would have shut down the machinery, but he had not done that. She listened more carefully, and in the quiet of the countryside she could hear that both the tractor and the corn picker were still running. At that moment she knew something was wrong. She ran for the car, got it going, and drove diagonally across the harvested rows until she came to where Louie was.

As the car came up alongside the tractor and picker, she saw Louie lying flat on the apron of the corn picker, struggling to extricate himself from the rollers. Minnie ran to the tractor, climbed up on the hitch, hoisted herself onto the fender, and pulled out the choke, thus killing the engine.

Louie was hardly conscious, but he was able to speak a little. There was a lot of blood spattered about, and he pointed to the place on his leg where it was coming from. Minnie knew she had to stanch the bleeding. She tore off her smock, buttons and all, and began ripping it into strips. She had to wrap several strips around his leg before the flow of blood eased. Then she helped Louie pull himself up. He leaned heavily on Minnie's shoulder, and they were both able to stand up. Louie was a tall, strapping man, but together they made it over to the passenger door of their big car. Louie dragged himself inside and onto the passenger seat.

"We've got to get to emergency," he said.

Worthington hospital was almost eighteen miles away. Minnie had never driven the car more than a mile or two away from their farm. Somehow she managed. She was the quiet one in the family, but, afraid that Louie would go into shock, she kept talking to him, and he responded. It was this, the doctors said later, that helped keep Louie alive.

Minnie drove as fast as she dared to the area hospital. She slowed down while crossing the railroad tracks, then turned onto Tenth Avenue. She saw the hospital up ahead and began honking the car horn. Hospital staff ran to meet them at the emergency entrance. They surrounded the car, opened the doors and went to work. They were able to stabilize Louie and save his leg.

* * * * * * * *

On Louie's first Sunday back in church, the congregation's relief was palpable. From then on, whenever I saw Louie and Minnie, I remembered how this brave and stalwart woman had helped her husband through a desperate time. Suddenly confronted with the most difficult of circumstances, she had kept her wits about her. At a time when others might have given in to despair, she kept going.

When I falter, I am grateful for my memories of her.

Worthington Municipal Hospital, c. 1950

First Station of the Cross

Ten Months

When I was a boy, our farmyard was nearly surrounded by large buildings, a grove of cottonwood trees that Sam and his brothers had planted during the early 1900s, and four quarter-mile long rows of evergreen trees that Dad and hired men planted in the 1940s. Those trees protected us from the strong winds that were common along Buffalo Ridge, and I felt safe there. Our barn survived when a tornado tore across the length of our farm and flattened the big barns of neighbors on both the east and west sides of our land.

When we stood in the middle of our yard, the only other farm we could see was across the road and half a mile to the southeast. Matt and Teresa Arens lived there. They were retired, and we farmed their land. To visit them, we walked the field path along the west side of the slough, turned south where it ended, and continued up the slope to their house on the crest of Buffalo Ridge. The slough was home to red-winged blackbirds and meadowlarks. The fence line along Ridge Road near the Arens end of the slough was a tangle of vines, and bluebirds made their nests in them.

After Mrs. Arens died, her body was brought back to their farm for the wake; family members and friends took turns keeping vigil. Our family had an assigned hour early in the morning. The parlor was filled with flowers and candles.

Not long after the funeral, Mr. Arens went to live with his son, and Dad rented the house for our hired man and his family. An apple orchard bordered the driveway, and Sister and I often played there with the neighbor children. I was old enough to help the hired man's wife, Patricia, at coffee time in the morning and tea time in the afternoon. If Mother was in the hospital, Patricia would make lunch for Dad and the men, and I would take it out to them. Patricia was not able to walk very well. Sometimes when my parents spoke of her, they said she was expecting. I did not know what that meant.

Late one afternoon, Patricia and her children drove over to our house. She did not get out of the car. Mother was at home and walked out to the gate to greet her. Marie and I followed.

A few minutes later Mother motioned us to come closer. Patricia said she and the children were driving into Wilmont to look at the sanctuary of their new church. All the furnishings had arrived, and the dedication service was scheduled to take place that weekend. She asked if I would like to go along. I wanted to know if the church had stained-glass windows, and she said it did. She told Mother I would be back in time for supper. Our family's church was out in the country on the way to Rushmore. It was small, white, and did not have stained-glass windows.

Patricia's church, Our Lady of Good Counsel, was in Wilmont. We had gone to the ground-breaking ceremony of the new Catholic church that would replace it. Occasionally we stopped past to watch as it changed from being a big hole in the ground into a large brick building. The last time I had seen it, the windows were covered with protective plywood and cardboard.

We drove into town and parked in front of the church. I got out and went around the car to hold the door for Patricia. She thanked me, and then I helped with the children – opening the church door, holding it for them – and we all went in. The side windows were still covered, but the stained-glass window at the front of the sanctuary was not. The late afternoon light streamed in from the west, and the colors were the most beautiful I had ever seen. No one else was there.

Our little group walked up to the altar rail. Patricia prepared to kneel. I moved to her side, and she balanced herself by resting her hand on my shoulder. There were a lot of candles burning in red glass vases. That surprised me because the rule at our house said lighted candles must never be left unattended.

Patricia said her rosary at the altar. I followed along, and when she came to "Holy Mary, Mother of God, pray for us sinners now and at the hour of our death," I said the words with her. Even though we were not Catholic, we always listened to the rosary program before Edward R. Murrow's radio news broadcast at 6:45 in the evening.

From the altar we went to the Stations of the Cross. Patricia knelt and prayed at every stop. It was difficult for her. There were quite a few stations, and I wondered if we would be going to all of them. Sometimes Patricia spoke in Latin; other times she prayed in English, and she stayed a long time at each station. Most of the children went to sit in the pews, and some of them fell asleep.

As we made our way through the church, the sun sank lower in the west. The light coming in the big window kept changing. I wished our Dutch church had stained-glass windows.

When we finished the Stations of the Cross, we went back to the altar. A priest appeared, came down to where we were standing, and blessed us all. Before we left the church, Patricia touched her fingers first to the holy water, then to my forehead, and said, "May the Lord bless and keep you, make the sun to shine upon you, and always grant you peace."

We went out to the car, arranged ourselves in it, and drove away. Back at the farm, I thanked Patricia, and she thanked me for helping her. Then she took her handkerchief and touched it to my forehead. Even though I was only a child, I remember thinking she was trying to tell me something, and that is why, after more than seven decades, I have written this down.

* * * * * * * *

Dad opened the kitchen door. My family was finishing supper. Mother brought my food from the stove to the table. I was given plenty of time to eat it. Sister cleared the table when I finished, and Mother went to the Frigidaire and brought back a big bowl of 24-hour salad with diced pineapple and green grapes in it. We ate dessert together. Marie and I were allowed to stay up and listen to George Burns and Gracie Allen on the radio. Our parents did not come in to join us. They remained in the kitchen, talking. Their voices were low, and I could not hear them well, but from time to time one of them, usually Mother, placed special emphasis on a word or two. I heard her say "ten months." I did not know what that meant, but it must have been important.

When Gracie Allen said "Good night," Dad came into the family room and said he was going to turn in. Marie asked him to play his harmonica so we could sing the "pretty red wing" song, but he said, "No, not tonight, maybe tomorrow." Then we all went upstairs to our bedrooms. When we were in our robes, we went out in the hall, seated ourselves on the sofa, and prayed together:

"Now I lay me down to sleep,

I pray the Lord my soul to keep.

If I should die before I wake,

I pray the Lord my soul to take."

Our parents kissed each of us on the forehead and said, "Good night, sleep tight." Then we went back to our rooms.

* * * * * * * *

At three o'clock the next morning a car drove on the yard. I heard the car door open and close, and then there was a knock at the front door. Dad went down to answer it. A few minutes later he came back upstairs and spoke with Mother. Then I heard the two of them coming down the hall. Mother stopped at Marie's room, Dad at mine.

They told us they were going over to the Arens house. If we needed anything, we should turn on the lights in our rooms, and Mil would come over from her little house next door to stay with us. Then they left.

Mil was making breakfast when Marie and I went downstairs the next morning. While we were eating, Dad returned and sat down in his usual place. He looked at us and said, "Patricia passed away early this morning. We'll go pick up Mother after breakfast. You won't be going to school today."

George Burns and Gracie Allen

St. Thomas Church, Leipzig

Grandpa

My cousin Ellen told me she was afraid of our grandfather. I was surprised to hear it. He died in 1949 when she was fifteen years old, and I was eleven, so I didn't have as many memories of him as she did, but I liked the memories I had. It made me sad to think that her memories of mother's dad were not all happy ones.

I also remember my grandmother. She died in 1944, when Mother was 33, and I was six. I do not remember the funeral, but I can recall a later time asking where had Grandma gone. Mother's eyes filled with tears as she looked at me and said, "Why, she's gone to heaven. Can't you hear her singing up there with all the other angels?"

* * * * * * * *

I do not know how Grandma and Grandpa met. My grandmother's maiden name was Rust. I always thought she came from Rust, a town near Vienna, famous for its storks. Franz Joseph Haydn lived near there for much of his life. He worked for the Esterhazy family in a castle with white walls and a red roof, not far from Austria's border with Hungary.

Grandpa was from Eisenach, in the German state of Thuringia, where Johann Sebastian Bach was born. It's a part of the world that is celebrated for its choirs and fine voices, like Wales in Great Britain. Grandpa never said much about his family, but I know from their papers that they were poor, and that was why he came to America.

Grandpa had also sung in a choir. He was, of course, old when I knew him, but not so old, and he still had a fine baritone voice. In 1948 my parents agreed to take him out to Oregon where most of his relatives had settled. He wanted to see them one last time before he died.

"Nobody lives forever," he said, and smiled. He had a gentle kind of humor that endeared him to us.

During that car trip, he taught us a song about an old man who lived "in a vine-covered shack in the mountains, bravely fighting the battle of time." When we finished memorizing that, he told us what Ellis Island was like when he arrived there on his way into this country. Long after his death, Aunt Lillie and Mother paid to have his name memorialized together with so many others who passed through Ellis Island.

On the way back to Minnesota, we learned another song. I still remember some of the words: "There's a lamp shining bright in the window, and I know that it's shining for me."

Like so many immigrants before him, Grandpa went to church on Sundays and tried to improve his English. He enjoyed the

134

singing, but before his English improved, he was mystified by a hymn that he thought said, "Hold the forks, the knives are coming." Later he learned the correct words were "Hold the fort, for I am coming."

* * * * * * * *

Mother remembered sitting next to her father in church, just listening to him sing. Grandma had a pedal organ and Grandpa played the violin. Mother's sisters had pianos in their homes. I remember where they were, and I can still hear Aunt Jennie singing in church. Her voice, like her laughter, was clear as a bell.

By the time I was ten, I had learned to play the pedal organ. Sometimes when I returned to Grandpa's house after my Saturday night piano lesson, Mother would whisper to me, "Go in and play the pedal organ for your grandfather." I would go into the living room and play the easy hymns from the hymnal. Sometimes Grandpa would take up his cane, cross the furnace grate in the floor between the dining room and the living room, and stand beside me. He would hum along with whatever it was I was playing. His voice was still rich and full. It had what some people call "color" in it, a good match for the deep blues and burgundies in the carpet.

* * * * * * * *

One day during the Oregon trip, we drove from Portland

(where Mother's cousins, Louise and Peggy, lived with their families) over to the ocean. Grandpa got out of the car and walked ahead of us, down a long wooden stairway and across the beach to where the waves were coming in. We waited. He stood out there for a long time. Then he took off his shoes and socks, placed them carefully on the sand, rolled his trousers up to the knees and walked out into the surf. A few minutes later he turned around and motioned for Sister and me to come join him.

We took off our sandals and socks and walked out to be next to him. Now and then a bigger wave rolled in, and soon our knees were wet. Marie and I shrieked and yelled, as children do. Then Grandpa wrapped his arms around our waists, picked us up, walked out even farther, and dangled us over the water.

By now our clothes were getting wet, but neither Mum nor Dad raised any objections to what was happening. It may be they were surprised that Grandpa was able to carry both of us at the same time. After a while, he took us back to where we had left our footwear, and we put ourselves back together.

* * * * * * *

I could feel the love my mother had for her father. Years later she told me how, when she was a little girl, she had enjoyed helping him in his basement workshop.

In 1914 her brother, Alan, was born. He was afflicted with

a genetic disorder, and he died when he was four years old. It was a terrible blow for the family. Grandpa had always whistled while he worked in his shop, but after the boy's death, the whistling stopped. Mother waited and waited for it to start up again, but it never did. She often said she thought her father's heart had broken when the little boy died.

Long after the Oregon trip, Mother told me that Grandpa said Marie and I had gladdened his heart, and he thanked her for making the effort to adopt us.

© Margo Harrison - stock.adobe.com

Pedal Organ

Russian Wolfhound

Willkie

I.   Fox Hunting

Mickey was my favorite hunting dog. He was a greyhound, but he was not gray. His color was unusual, something like sandalwood. I've forgotten the name of Marie's greyhound. He was a light gray. These two dogs teamed with Dad's wolfhound, Willkie. If the foxes of Nobles County had been able to name the ten dogs they *least* wanted to meet on a day when there was new-fallen snow on the ground, it's likely these three dogs would have been at the top of the list.

Fox hunting with dogs is not something that is done primarily for sport. There are compelling reasons for farmers to keep the fox population under control. It is regarded as necessary work. One fox can kill dozens of chickens in an hour. Anyone who raises chickens for a living knows that co-existence between chickens and foxes requires some rules. It would be nice if foxes could read warning signs telling them to go hunt rabbits, gophers, and grouse rather than chickens, but that is not going to happen.

For shepherds in the Alps and the Pyrenees, who must protect their sheep from wolves, and foresters everywhere who try to save young trees from marauding deer, it is an ongoing battle. Many people do not like hearing that municipalities hire sharpshooters to go out in the early-morning hours to cull the deer population, but most agree that something has to be done. They just don't want to know about it. That's why sharpshooters use silencers on their guns. Out of earshot, out of mind.

* * * * * * * *

Fox hunting with dogs is not done much anymore. It died out on its own. People never had to organize protests to stop it. Today there are fewer family farms, and most of those remaining do not have chicken coops. One no longer sees egg trucks making their rounds out in the country, but foxes still go out on chilly nights to seek food for their young. More and more of them are finding what they need in urban areas.

Dad hunted foxes with his dogs. He regarded it as a struggle between equals. He never carried a gun. He did not take sides when his wolfhound matched skills with a fox. When the fox got away, as it often did, Dad would go home and say, "Well, Mary, the fox out-foxed us today." For a time in the 1940s, foxes were hunted from the air. Dad and his friends regarded that as unsportsmanlike. They worked with Minnesota Governor Luther W. Youngdahl's commission to have that practice stopped.

When the hunt was over, Dad would invite his friends and

their families to our house for supper, and people would tell their favorite fox stories. Hunters have hearty appetites. After a day spent tramping across the fields, the late evening suppers were memorable for good food and camaraderie. It was, I think, country living at its best. For us, eating and hunting went together, like a horse and carriage. Those days are gone now – like so much else, a thing of the past.

Minnesota Historical Society

Luther W. Youngdahl

Fox Tracks in Snow

II.   The Chase

When I was a boy, I looked forward to Saturday mornings. I hoped the phone would ring because it was often a farmer calling to say a fox had gotten into his poultry barn the night before and killed a lot of chickens. He would ask Dad to come with the dogs to track down the animal. Dad would call some friends and neighbors, and they would get up a hunting party. Usually they gathered at our place to map out their strategy, and then it was off to the farm where the fox had done its reprehensible work.

A hunt had the best chance of catching a fox if there was snow on the ground. Snow the night before was best, as fresh snow makes it easier to track the fox. Without good snow, hunters had to work harder to find traces of the fox that had done the killing. In some ways it was like police work. One had to pay careful attention to detail. Some hunters, like detectives, are better at doing that than others. And it is easier to catch a thief or a fox if one has the help of a good dog or two.

Once the fox trail was found, the dogs would get on the scent and follow it until the animal was sighted, and then the chase began. The hounds would try to run the animal to ground. When the fox began to tire, it would sometimes try to take cover, or hide somewhere, often in a fox hole. When dogs confront a raccoon, it might try to climb a tree. It is unusual for a fox to try to climb a tree, but it happens occasionally. It is either that, or prepare to fight.

Greyhounds are smaller and lighter than wolfhounds, but they can run faster. They are usually the first to get close to the fox, but greyhounds are afraid of foxes. Most are reluctant to tangle with them. They prefer to hang back, keeping their distance, while continuing to work at tiring the animal. They wait for the wolfhound to catch up and then let it take over.

This is the crucial part of the hunt. Foxes are smaller than hunting dogs, but they are wily and can be vicious. At this point, it is anybody's guess who the winner will be, the wolfhound or the fox. It all depends on the skill that each animal brings to the occasion.

As the years passed, Willkie earned a reputation for being very good at what he did, and we were proud to call him ours.

Worthington Daily Globe

Reward for the
safe return
of our wolfhound.
Herman Elsing,
Rushmore, Minnesota,
Telephone: 4646

III.   Stolen

One Sunday after church, Marie went out to the kennel and then came running back to tell us that Willkie was not there. Dad found it hard to believe; Mother went to lie down on grandma's fainting couch. As everyone knows, pets are sometimes almost like members of the family, and that's the way it was with us.

Although Dad didn't say so right away, I think he knew at once what had happened. Willkie had been stolen. The sheriff's deputy came out and suggested that Willkie had run away. Dad scoffed at this idea and told the lawman in no uncertain terms that in more than fifty years no dog had ever run away from our farm. The deputy apologized, stayed around for a while, and left convinced that Dad was right. Willkie had been stolen.

We placed an ad in the county paper and offered a reward for Willkie's safe return. As a result of the reward offer, our telephone began to ring at all hours of the day and night. I remember once at midnight a farmer who lived far away from us, almost in Iowa, called and said he had our dog penned up in his barn.

"Will you please come and get it?" he asked. We dressed and left at once.

There were no electric lights in that barn, so we had to use a flashlight. I remember shining the light into a pen and seeing a collie. Dad cleared his throat and said, "You know, we're looking for our wolfhound; his coat is not so thick and long as a collie's." He gave the man a tip anyway. When we were back in the car, Dad said, "You never know who might come up with your next best lead."

We had to deal with many a "wild goose" chase, and it wore us down. One day the phone rang, Mother answered, and the caller said he had seen our dog. We had heard that line before. Mother asked, "What makes you think it's our dog?" The man answered, "Well, I have a five-foot fence around my cattle yard; our dogs just crawl under it, but your dog jumped over it." *

"Stay where you are," Mother said. "We're coming."

Dad called his farmer-pilot friend, Bill Boldt, asked him to fly to the address we'd been given, and to look for Willkie from the air.

"If you see any sign of him, dip your wings a couple times above the spot, and I'll try to get there. The farmer thinks Willkie is in the corn field."

When Dad reached the farm, Bill's plane was circling overhead. Dad went out to the corn field and began walking up and down the rows. Bill in the airplane and Dad on the ground searched for a sign of Willkie for a long time. It was beginning to get dark, but then the wings of the plane dipped and dipped again. Dad waved. Bill flew as low as he could – right over Dad's head – and tossed an empty ice cream carton out of the plane. Dad saw it fall, ran and found it. Bill had written a note: "Running low on fuel, have to go

---

* A dog that's not good at jumping fences can hold up a hunt. All our dogs were good jumpers.

home. Willkie is circling around you in the corn field. Good luck."

Dad was tired, but he kept going, calling for Willkie until his voice gave out. The sun was setting. Suddenly, behind him, Dad heard the corn stalks rustling. Just as he was about to turn around, Willkie jumped full on Dad's back, knocking him to the ground. Willkie was not a lightweight dog, but Dad was over six feet tall and weighed more than 200 pounds. Apparently, Willkie needed to be certain he had found the right man. That's why he'd circled around Dad for so long. Having finally assured himself that he had found his owner, there was no holding him back.

Courtesy FMS

Small Airplane

Wicked Witch of the West

Wicked Witch of the West [*]

The District 84 schoolhouse is history now. We had a radio, but television did not reach us until the early 1950s. There was a movie theater in Wilmont, but we didn't go there often. After our parents made the mistake of taking us to see "Snake Pit," Mother said, "We'll never go there again." Compared with the way things are now, life in those days was simple, at least for those of us who lived in the country.

One day in 1950 the Nobles County Library Association announced a contest for sixth-graders. The rules were easy. Contestants had to dress up as one of their favorite characters and memorize a paragraph or two of something the character had said in a book. The program would take place at a school in Worthington.

I was eager to take part, and Mother agreed to make the costume. I wanted to be Daniel Boone or Davy Crockett, I forget which. Mother bought a red and black plaid shirt, tied a blue bandana around my neck, and finished the job with chaps and a leather vest. Making the "coonskin" cap took a little longer. I found something to read and memorized it, but I had only been in church programs, so there wasn't much in the way of expression in my presentation. I

---

[*] Seen in the MGM movie *The Wizard of Oz* (1939)

hoped the audience would like my cap, but I worried that the fox tail might fall off.

When we arrived at the school in Worthington, the librarians lined us up off-stage, but from the side, we could see the performers. I stood there with my hands clasped behind my back, and waited.

The boy ahead of me had memorized a rant by Long John Silver, and when it was over, there was thunderous applause. Later, when I finished, there was applause as well, but not so much. I bowed and returned to my seat.

No sooner had the curtains closed than they opened again, and we got the shock of our young lives. A girl about my age, dressed all in black with a lot of pearl buttons and wearing high-topped shoes, rushed out – arms akimbo – to the center of the stage. She was wearing a big black hat, high and pointed, with a floppy brim. Her wig, made of long twisty black hair, probably came from her pony's mane. Obviously a witch, she scared everybody, and some of the smaller children began to cry. That face, with lots of black makeup around the eyes and on both sides of its nose, was, I think, the most fearsome thing any of us had ever laid eyes on. She wore thick, black-rimmed glasses; her lips were painted the bloodiest red imaginable, and she was grinning jagged teeth to rival those of any Dracula.

As if all that was not enough for the audience to contend with, this witch hopped, jumped, and stomped around the stage like a demon possessed. She snapped and cackled like a giant popcorn popper gone berserk. And then the odd noises started. We heard what at first sounded like gibberish on speed. Her voice was a cross between a screech and fingernails scratching on a blackboard. It had obviously been rehearsed for the express purpose of setting one's teeth on edge and making every hair on one's head stand on end. After a while, we heard her say, "I'll get you, my pretty, and your little dog, too." This was followed by "Something with poison in it, I think. With poison in it." And then came that laugh, "Ha ha ha ha ha!"

Well, I'm here to tell you she tripped our wires! She was, in a word, fierce, like the evil one incarnate. She took our breath away, and we were all left speechless, except for the judges. When they came out from behind the curtain – holding their sides – and the applause subsided, they pronounced her to be the wickedest witch the West had ever seen. They proclaimed her winner of the competition. Certainly no one in the audience that day would have disagreed with their unanimous decision. Like Long John Silver, the performer who had preceded us, she had "shivered our timbers" right down to the foundations.

Pheasant

Greg and Katie

Greg and Katie were Dad and Mother's best friends. Any one of them could look at a restaurant menu and know what the other three would order. Sometimes they bought clothes for one another, or wallpaper. And once, in 1951, they astonished themselves and the other guests by arriving at a party in two brand-new Mercury cars, both the same color: ocean green.

Greg and Katie were Catholic. We were not. Sometimes we saw nuns at their house when we went to visit. They usually came back to the farm in the fall of the year, during pheasant season. They told us there were no pheasants at the monastery school where they taught. Marie – almost four years younger than I – wondered if God had forgotten to leave pheasants at the monastery.

"No, I don't think so," I said, "Pheasants try to hide from people, so that may be why the nuns have never seen them. It's only hunters who see pheasants, because hunters go out in groups called hunting parties and try to flush pheasants from their hiding places. That's the best time to see pheasants. Also, hunters need guns, and I don't think anyone at the monastery is allowed to have guns. We've been going with Greg and Katie and their children to celebrate feast days at the monastery church for a long time, and I have never seen guns there."

"But I've seen guns there," said Marie. Dad asked where they were. She said they were painted on the walls with the shepherds and the sheep.

"No," Dad said, "you must have seen staffs. Shepherds use them to herd the sheep."

"Oh, I know why there are no pheasants at the monastery," Sister said.

"Why?" I asked.

"It's because the monastery is in the Great Mississippi River Basin National Forest [sic], and pheasants don't live in forests. They live in corn fields. They would probably starve to death if they had to live in forests."

I wasn't so sure about that, but I had heard Effie tell Mother that Marie was precocious. I thought that had something to do with big words, and Little Sister certainly did know a lot of big words, so I decided Effie was probably right.

* * * * * * *

The nuns told us Katie was supposed to have been a nun, too, but then, at the age of sixteen, she met Greg, and from then on the two of them were inseparable. For a while, Katie's parents continued to hope that she, the youngest of their children, would follow in the footsteps of her aunts and become a nun, but as time went by, they gave up on that idea. They recognized and accepted beautiful when they saw it.

When Katie turned eighteen, her parents gave her a party in the newest room of their house, although it wasn't quite finished. When it came time to sing "Happy Birthday," Katie's mother nodded to her and Katie sat down at the piano. Greg appeared with his violin and took his place beside her. First they played "Happy Birthday" as a piano-violin duet, and after that everyone sang. The group wished Katie a happy birthday. Her father brought in a huge white cake, lit the eighteen candles, and Katie blew them out with one breath. Everyone cheered. Katie's mother looked at her, smiled, and said, "What do you wish for, dear Katie?"

At that moment Katie knew it would be all right to ask the question she had been harboring for what seemed like an eternity. She turned to Greg, he took her hand in his, and they walked over to face Katie's parents. "I want to marry Greg," she said.

Her mother embraced her, and her father kissed Katie on the forehead. Both parents shook hands with Greg. Permission had been given. Greg and Katie married and had six children, three girls and three boys. All of them were musical.

* * * * * * * *

Thirty-five years later Mother wrote to say that Greg and Katie had died. They had both been ill for a long time and were sharing a suite in a local hospital. At seven o'clock on a Monday morning, Greg rang for Katie, but she did not answer. When the nurse went over to tell him that Katie could no longer hear, she found that he, too, had passed away. When told that Greg and Katie were dead, Katie's mother sighed and said, "For them it is a blessing. Neither could have lived without the other."

Courtesy Jerry Swenson

Heiligenkreuz, Austria

Sam Elsing Barn, c. 1914

Bad Egg

Junior high school kids who lived on farms did not have clubhouses the way their town classmates did. We had hideouts. Mine was the best of all possible hiding places, but it was small. There was only room for one person, and that one person was me.

Our farm had a big barn. The whole family, and even some of the neighbors, seemed to take pride in it. Whenever the talk was about barns, someone was sure to say, "That barn is one of the largest in the county." My grandfather Sam and his two brothers built it in the early 1900s. Dad and his brothers were children at that time. They helped their father and uncles by fetching and carrying the myriad things that are needed for a project of that size.

Most people we knew called it a Dutch barn, and we were a Dutch family. Both the big barn and the auxiliary barn had Dutch doors. Each door was divided into two parts, upper and lower. Either part could be left open while the other remained closed. Some of the upper doors were left open during warm weather, but most of the time both doors were shut. Sam liked the farmstead to look neat. He considered it bad form to leave a door open without good reason.

One morning Dad and his brothers and sisters forgot to close the big barn door when they left for school in their pony cart.

When Sam noticed the open door, he saddled his horse, rode after the children, and told them to turn around, return home, and close that door. The youngsters did as they were told. From then on, they remembered to close doors after themselves.

* * * * * * * *

Until Dad married Mother, he said the barn had a "hipped" roof, but she told him the dictionary called it a gambrel roof. Because she was a schoolteacher, he took her word for it and tried to adapt his nomenclature accordingly, but sometimes he forgot and said "hipped." It is not incorrect.

Visitors sometimes called it a "dogleg" roof. It's easy to see why. All one has to do is look at the hind leg of a hound dog. The dogleg one finds on the fairway of a golf course also has a sharp angle.

The pitch of the lower part of a gambrel roof is steeper than the pitch of the upper part. Our barn had a dormer door in the lower part of the roof. Every year in August the door was opened, and oats for the horses was elevatored up into the barn where it poured down into the oats bin above the part of the barn where the horses were stabled. Horses eat oats as well as hay. Their stalls are bedded down with straw.

When the oats bin in the barn was full, the elevator was moved to the granary in preparation for the corn harvest in early October. It stayed there until the following August when the cycle began again.

The dormer door was not used during the rest of the year. There was no reason for anyone to go up there. It was beyond the reach of any ladder we had. The dormer space with its solid wood floor resting on beams was the perfect place for a hideout. From this vantage point, I could pretend to be a pirate on a ship's forecastle looking out through his telescope at the sea.

One day a hired man called down and said, "Wow, it's like being between the devil and the deep blue sea, except it's hay I see below me, not water. I'm afraid to look up lest I see the devil himself, lose my balance, and fall in." It would have been a long way down.

There was a catwalk from the front of the barn to the back of it that passed along the rafters. Perpendicular to it, there was a three-board extension with a guide rope that led over to the dormer door, like a gangplank. Whenever I went up to my perch, I pulled the first board of the gangplank in after me, so no one could follow. When I was ready to go back down, it was easy to slide that board back into position.

As the years passed, I spent a lot of time in my hideout. It was my favorite place for reading, a refuge all my own. A small piece of siding was missing from the dormer wall, so there was good light and a clear view of the lane that came in from the road, circled the windmill, passed by the house, and then led back out to the road. If anyone drove on the yard, I could look down and see them. When

Mother rang the dinner bell, I could see her, too.

* * * * * * *

We were a church-going family. Like their father Sam before them, Dad and his brother John were presiding elders of the congregation. Mother was the Sunday school superintendent for almost forty years. She was there every Sunday except for the times when she was living at the hospital. Cousin Mil substituted for her.

Through all those years, I remember missing church only twice or maybe three times. That was because I had a fever, and Mother thought it best if I stayed at home to rest. That's the way it was one Sunday morning when I was twelve years old. Soon after the rest of the family left for church, I began to feel better and tried taking my temperature, but I don't think the reading was accurate. I ate some of the breakfast left on the table and then went out to the barn to read in my retreat.

Half an hour later I heard the cattle braying out in the corral. That was unusual, it almost never happened. Every September when the calves arrived from our cousin's ranch in eastern Colorado, they would bray for a few days. Dad called it "crying." After that they settled into their new home, and the braying stopped.

I waited, thinking that a stray dog was passing by, but the braying continued. The cattle were agitated by something. The feed lot was on the other side of the barn, so I went down to the lower part

Windmill c. 1950

of the hayloft and looked out the clerestory windows on the other side of the building.

The steers were milling about, jostling one another, and charging into the big steel gates that enclosed the stockyard. I still could not see anything out of the ordinary, but something was wrong. I waited a little longer and noticed something whitish – a puff of smoke – out in the pole barn. Someone was out there smoking a cigarette, something you don't ever want to do on a farm like ours. I remember the time Dad found one of the farmhands smoking in the barn. Dad told him to pack his bags and be gone by sundown. No questions were asked because no explanation was needed. Everyone knew the rules. The man went to his tenant house, told his family about the move, and they were gone from our lives before dark.

* * * * * * * *

I knew this was serious. More puffs of smoke followed and then, in the shadows, someone stood up. A young man carrying a shotgun came out into the sunlight. I had seen this fellow before and knew who he was. He hadn't been allowed to ride the school bus because he bullied the children. He lived somewhere north of town, two or three miles away. He had worked for us one summer, but Dad had to "let him go" because he was neither reliable nor trustworthy. Ever afterward, he hated us. Dad called him a bad egg. His vile behavior caused our family heartache.

I moved to the shadow and waited. Our farm dog, a collie we called Turtle, trotted up to the fence below. He wouldn't bark unless I gave the signal.

Suddenly the smoker began to wail like a banshee, spooking the cattle even more. Then he began beating the animals nearest him with a big stick he had picked up somewhere. Panic ensued, and the herd began running in circles. As the yelling continued, the steers broke ranks and headed for the gates. Some of the animals stumbled and fell, or were knocked down and couldn't get up again. In quick succession, the pipe gates went crashing to the ground, and more than a hundred head of Aberdeen Angus broke out into the south pasture.

At the same time, our three hunting dogs – who had somehow escaped the confines of their kennel – came leaping over the board fence next to the silos. They saw the man and went after him. The intruder stopped his noise-making and jumped over the feed bunks in the hope of getting into the barn before the dogs fell upon him. He knew what would happen if they caught him. Still carrying the shotgun, he reached to open the barn door, then looked up and saw me. He knew I had seen him harrying the cattle. He had nothing more to lose. I did not doubt for a minute that he was prepared to use the gun on me.

What a mistake! With all the commotion and uproar, I had forgotten myself. The cattle stampeded across the pasture, tore through a double barbed-wire fence, and were out on the road. Several cars and a semi-trailer truck began honking their horns as if there were no tomorrow. One car veered into the ditch and landed on its side. As if all that was not enough to worry about, the bad egg was now in the barn, and he had a gun.

Two ladders led up to the hayloft, and my nemesis was standing next to one of them. From there, he could watch the other ladder. He would not leave that spot because he had to make certain I did not use a ladder to get out of the loft.

I was trapped and had to think of something fast. With almost no first-hand knowledge to draw on, I guessed that the shotgun was not as powerful a weapon as a .22-caliber rifle. It could not pierce boards as thick as those from the oats chute that walled the dormer space, i.e., my hideout. If I could get back to the dormer and into the space between the wall and the dormer threshold, I thought I might have a chance, but first I had to get up to the catwalk.

The barn was filled with bales of hay. They were roped and secured in sections that almost touched the rafters in some places. If I could reach the catwalk, it would be possible to get to the gangplank without being seen from below.

That was my plan. I crept slowly and carefully through the alleyway between the bale stacks, always checking to see if the gunman still had his eye on the other ladder and his back to me.

I climbed to the catwalk and followed it to the gangplank. I stepped onto the first board, and when I reached the second one, I turned around, lifted the first board, and carried it to the dormer space.

Just as I was about to place it on the rafters, it slipped from my grasp and clattered down along the outside of the oats bin wall. It hit the hay with a whooshing sound.

In what seemed like a flash, the gunman appeared at the far end of the barn. He got up on the catwalk and began making his way in my direction. I could see by the care he took that he was scared and afraid of falling.

I crawled into the space between the wall and the dormer door.

My assailant reached the turnoff and pivoted to face the spot where I was hiding. He was standing sideways on the narrow catwalk, and that rendered his balance more precarious. He looked down and saw that the first section of the gangplank was missing. He knew I had removed it. A vicious malignity hardened every line of his face. For the first time since entering the barn, he spoke, but he did not say much, and most of it was monosyllabic. When he stopped, an eerie silence settled over the cavernous space.

During those moments, I thought my heart was going to break out of my rib cage into the open air, but I stayed crouched between the wall and the threshold. Through a tiny crack between the top two wall boards I saw the man raise the shotgun and aim it in my direction. He was trembling. I hoped the shotgun blast would not be powerful enough to carry halfway across the width of the barn.

With no rafter or other support to lean against to steady himself, the gunman was shaking. He was trying hard to concentrate on what he was doing. Just as he was about to pull the trigger, the board on which he was standing made a sharp cracking sound. It startled him. His body jerked violently forward and back, like a stick puppet being yanked about on a string.

Oats began trickling down from the high sidewalls of the half-empty grain bin. Suddenly the creaking board broke in two. An avalanche of oats cascaded downward. The space filled with dust and chaff that was almost as thick as suspended flour.

At that moment what looked to me like an electric shock convulsed the interloper. He lost his balance, fell into the torrent of oats, and was swept into the pit.

I waited for the cascading oats to stop, and finally it did. When the dust settled, I raised my head a little and looked for the gunman, but the oats had not given him quarter. I crossed myself and waited.

* * * * * * * *

The honking had stopped. The dogs were quiet. I heard voices outside, and then someone opened the barn door.

Herd of Black Angus

Brush, Colorado, postmark

Colorado

I.   Brush Fire

Like everything else on the high plains of eastern Colorado, the brush fires stay close to the ground. We could smell the fire before we saw it. Brush fires can spread rapidly, sometimes moving across the land as fast as a car. When cousin Walt saw fire on the horizon, he said, "There's not enough time to drive around it; we'll have to go through it." And then, in a voice that had to be obeyed, he said, "Get down and stay down." We did as we were told.

We were in a four-door Hudson. It was two-tone, chocolate and cream, like the colors in some Pullman cars. Hudsons were popular with ranchers in the 1950s because they were big, fast, and had a low center of gravity. One had to step up and then down to get into them.

Years later whenever someone said, "Put the pedal to the metal," I remembered what happened next. The car took off and sped toward the fire. When the smoke surrounded us, it was not heavy and black, but whitish and wispy, so we were not driving completely blind, but it was scary, nevertheless. Before one could say "jolly rancher," we were on the other side, racing the wind. Soon the stunted trees and low buildings of the ranch came into view.

Walt honked the horn as we rocketed past the gateposts. At first surprised, I soon realized what was happening. The firebreak around the ranch buildings had been disked the day before, but there had not been time enough to do the firebreak around the church and the few houses near it. That's where we were heading. A few minutes later, the car stopped at the church shed. Walt jumped out, started the tractor, pulled the disk over to the firebreak, and got to work.

By that time the woman and children who lived in the house nearest the church were in the Hudson. The ranch foreman got behind the wheel. Cousin Eleanor in her car and her brother-in-law in his pickup arrived. Walt shouted for them to leave the pickup and follow the Hudson. It all went like clockwork.

* * * * * * * *

The fire did not jump the firebreak. It died out. By evening everything was back to normal, except for the acrid smell of smoke that hung in the air.

Dad asked why Mrs. Boone was still in that house when everyone thought the family had moved away. Walt said her husband had brought her and the children out for the day and had then driven back to Denver. We told him the woman and her children – none of them – had said a single word while they were in the car with us. Walt said, "Well, you know, there's a reason for that," and then he told us this story.

II.   Closer to God

The Boone family had rented the house a few years earlier. They had moved out to the country, they said, because the city was too wicked. They chose the house nearest the church because they wanted to be "closer to God."

The church congregation was small, elderly, and shrinking. Its few members had welcomed the newcomers with open arms. The church re-started its Sunday school just for the children in the new family. When regular school started, the parishioners saw that the youngsters needed some extra clothes. They gathered up some nice things from their grown children's closets and gave them to the new neighbors.

When Christmas came, the ladies of the church put together a big basket of fruit and canned goods for the family. They placed it under the church Christmas tree, together with a small toy for each child and some board games. The family sent a thank-you note.

The next year the children told their Sunday school teacher they did not need any fruit or vegetables, but they would like some video games. The church ladies checked their closets, found some nice toys, and put them under the church tree for distribution after the Christmas program. Then they waited for a thank-you, but it never appeared.

When the third Christmas came around, the ladies received a note from the family with specific requests, including prices and the names of stores where the items could be found. The ladies resumed their usual practice of fruit, some canned goods, and a small toy or two for each child.

The family stopped attending church services. Later that year the janitor found BBs on the floor of the sanctuary and saw the holes they had made in the stained-glass windows. There was a package of store-bought cookies for the family at Christmas time that year, but no one came to pick it up.

Philip Pilosian/Shutterstock.com

Hudson Car, c. 1950

Sopwith Camel

Flat Tire

One day near the end of her life, Mother and I were talking about her aunts and uncles. She mentioned an aunt whose name was not familiar to me.

"Why haven't I heard that name before?" I asked.

"Because the family wanted to forget her," Mother answered.

"Why did they want to do that?"

"Because of the awful way she died," Mother said, speaking so softly I could hardly hear her.

I wanted to ask a direct question, but Mother's eyes filled with tears. She was haunted by her aunt's death, and I waited a few minutes before asking, "Can you tell me about it?"

Through her tears, Mother said, "Yes, Aunt Edwina did some strange things, but I would like for her to be remembered because she was always kind to me."

Mother paused, took a deep breath, poured more coffee, and said she hoped I would remember that kindness.

Here is the story I wrote in memory of Mother's eccentric aunt. It is told in Mother's voice, but it is fiction. Almost the only thing I know for certain about my great aunt is how she died:

After Aunt Edwina lost the use of her legs in a boating accident, she invited our family – your Grandpa and Grandma, Lillie and me – to live in her house on the Wisconsin side of the St. Croix River. She moved herself and her cats into a cottage farther along the riverbank trail, but not out of our sight. She was afraid of fire.

By the time I started high school, there were some problems with this arrangement. Edwina was distancing herself from us. She guarded her privacy with a ferociousness that surprised and confounded your grandparents. Grandpa said she was "a little on the odd side," but he said it kindly. Grandma said it was "way too much and not helpful." They both loved Edwina dearly and did everything they could to make her life near us as agreeable as possible.

* * * * * * * *

Edwina's only child, a captain in the U.S. Army Air Service, was shot down over France during the Great War and died in the crash. Today we call it World War I. The others in his squadron made it back to base safely and survived the war. They visited us in Wisconsin in the mid-1920s. They always said they were alive because Edwina's son had given his life for them, and they were grateful.

* * * * * * * *

The Sopwith Camels[*] had been on a routine training mission when enemy aircraft, out-numbering them two to one, swooped down from the gray skies

---

[*] "A metal fairing over the gun breeches, intended to protect the guns from freezing at altitude, created a 'hump,' and it was this feature that led pilots to refer to the aircraft by the name Camel." (Wikipedia)

178

above the town of Meaux and attacked them. The right-hand side wing of the captain's biplane took the first hit and burst into flames followed by heavy black smoke. In seconds the formation broke up and chaos followed. Undaunted by the fire and smoke that threatened to envelop both him and his plane, the captain stayed at the controls and began a high-stakes game of bluff and nerves, with the idea of keeping the attackers' attention focused on himself. He took over the space between his plane and the slower enemy aircraft and made it his own.

With what seemed like insouciant ease to those who witnessed it, he darted back and forth in front of and around the larger, but less agile, enemy planes, his Sopwith's machine gun firing all the while. Again and again, in close quarters, he put himself and his plane at great risk, but succeeded in keeping the enemy at bay. Within minutes they were thrown into disarray and retreated into the clouds from which they had descended a short time before.

The attackers paid a heavy price for the brief encounter with the Americans. Half a dozen enemy planes had been destroyed, all but one of them put out of commission by the captain. Somehow, against great odds, he was able to keep his stricken craft in the air long enough to finish what the enemy had started. By diverting their attention from his fellow pilots, the captain had given the men time enough to get away. By looping the loop and seeming to be here, there, and everywhere at once, he had almost singlehandedly saved the Sopwith Camels and the men who were in them. And then, just when the captain could see that his command was out of danger, his plane bucked, veered sharply to the right, and went down in a blaze of orange glory.

The rest of the squadron returned to Paris, their planes undamaged and the young lieutenants who flew them unharmed. They carried with them the memory of a drama valiantly fought that went far beyond anything they had ever seen or dreamed of. The airmen never forgot their captain, and when, years later, his ashes were recovered and returned to the United States, they invited Edwina to go with them to Washington, D.C., to visit his grave.

Much to our astonishment, she accepted.

* * * * * * * *

A few months later, the airman Edwina liked best arrived in Wisconsin with his wife, and, together with Edwina, they took the train out to Washington and back again. After that, Auntie continued to withdraw from the world around her, and this caused our family, your grandmother in particular, a lot of pain.

In the late 1920s, the airman's wife wrote asking if they would be welcome to visit Wisconsin again. Grandma walked the letter down to the cottage and placed it in the pass-through on the porch. That evening the "Mail Waiting" flag went up, and I went to fetch the reply. It told us to tell the airmen that their captain's mother was dead. The next day the flag went up again. This time the note said if the airman and his wife ever set foot in Wisconsin again, Auntie would cross our names out of her will.

* * * * * * * *

Life went on like this for several years. Lillie and I finished high school and went on to college at the University of Wisconsin in River Falls, ten miles away. We continued to live at home.

During all that time Auntie wrote a note once a week, and we wrote back, always making sure to ask if there was anything we could do for her. Two or three times a month she left a shopping list in the pass-through. Every Monday she left her "to do" laundry in a bag that fit between the doors. It was always returned to her the next day, redolent of lavender. Every other day or so there was a small plastic bag filled with the latest contents of her wastepaper basket. She never opened the curtains on the side of the cottage that faced our house, so we never saw her.

One winter day her note asked us to telephone her physician friend, a man with whom she had gone to high school. He came to see her that same day. After he left the cottage, he stopped at our house. It soon became apparent that he had been sworn to secrecy. He did not tell us anything about our relative, even though he must have known that this made things even more difficult for us. Grandpa asked him about Edwina's high-tech, rubber-tired and motorized wheelchair. The doctor said it was "still going strong." He added that "Eddie" never forgot to plug it into the Briggs and Stratton generator at night, and then he left. He said he would visit again later that month.

* * * * * * * *

A few weeks later, the doctor's car stopped at the cottage; minutes after that, he came over to our house, knocked on the door, and told us that "Eddie" was dead. Suddenly trembling, and in tears, Grandma asked, "When did she die?"

"Oh," he said, looking around as if he had just received word of something important, "maybe two or three weeks ago."

After notifying the mortuary, he asked if it would be all right for him to let the cats out, and would we mind looking after them? We nodded our heads, giving wordless consent. He walked back to Auntie's cottage and waited. No one mentioned the cause of death.

The mortuary team arrived within the hour and took the body away. Soon after they left, the cleaning service came to fumigate the cottage. They told Grandpa they would return the next day to open all the doors and windows and air the place out. Once that was accomplished, we would be allowed to go in.

Later that week some of the cats began appearing at our doorstep. They were not afraid of us, and Grandpa said they were "bright-eyed and bushy-tailed."

* * * * * * * *

The cause of Edwina's death remained a mystery; however, Lillie liked mysteries. She had published one of her own, and another was ready to go to the printer, "just like Dorothy Sayers," she said.

One day Lillie told me she had figured out what she believed had happened to Auntie. She asked if I remembered that Grandpa had not allowed us to take Aunt Edwina's wheelchair up to the storage shed.

"Yes, that's right," I answered, "he told us it was broken."

"Exactly," she continued, "but a few days later we noticed that someone had forgotten to lock the shed; we went in and found the wheelchair cleaned, polished, and in good condition."

"Except for that one very flat tire," I said.

"Yes, it left black rubber burn marks on the kitchen floor," Lillie added, "as if it had been spinning in place for a long time."

But how and why this had happened, we did not know. And we had no way of finding out what things had looked like in the kitchen when Auntie's physician friend found her body.

At that moment, I realized what had happened. Without altering my tone of voice, I said, "You can't put that in one of your mysteries."

Lillie, always the pinnacle of calm, looked at me and said, "No, of course not. I wouldn't do that. My readers will have to solve it for themselves."

I looked at my brainy sibling, and from somewhere deep inside me the line "Easy for you to say, Horatio," came to mind.

Under my breath, I said, "I don't think your readers are going to like that."

Briggs & Stratton generator

Tom Sawyer and Huckleberry Finn

Charleston, South Carolina*

Nineteen hundred sixty-five was not a good year for Angel Cooper. Her husband died of something so unfashionable that she could not bear the prospect of seeing his obituary in *The New York Times*. Whenever it crossed her mind that she would no longer see the name Cooper linked with her late husband's club, the Colonnato, on her special invitations, she could almost feel the lines on her forehead deepen.

Angel had long ago given up any hope of being rescued from obscurity by her daughter, Priscilla. Not only had her darling child married outside the club, she had gone to work for Charleston County as a nurse. She had been appointed Director of Nursing, true enough, but still, to think of Priscilla with her Pilgrim name working for the county, well, it just rankled. For those who didn't know any better, what her daughter was doing might seem to have been taken from the same bottom drawer as being on the dole, and certainly no one would ever want to countenance that.

If only Priscilla had tried a little harder to find a husband

---

* This story began as an entry ("Three Rivers") in my journal during the eight years in the 1990s when my daughter lived in the Carolinas, first in Charleston SC, and then in Durham NC. A few years ago, a friend from Charleston gave me a reason to finish it.

within the club, surely there would have been someone suitable enough from among Charleston's finest, but it was too late for that. What's done is done.

How could Angel possibly put a good face on the fact that Priscilla had not only married a stockbroker, but he was a New York City stockbroker! As if that were not enough of a cross to bear, this person continued to live in New York, while commuting on weekends to South Carolina where he managed to father five children (including twins) in six years. That pricey nurses' academy where they enrolled Priscilla had a lot to answer for, in Angel's opinion. After all, weren't they supposed to teach young girls in white uniforms the facts of life?

Once these annual deliveries began, Angel had hoped the whole lot of them would skedaddle off for Manhattan. Wouldn't the tall buildings up there make it difficult for people to determine how many children their neighbors had? But no, they all stayed in Charleston, and – as if to add insult to injury – the stockbroker continued his weekly commute, and that, of course, always provided the ticketmaster's wife with something new to talk about at her Tuesday morning bridge parties.

No, as far as Angel was concerned, 1965 had signaled the beginning of her decline.

* * * * * * * *

And then, early one morning as Angel's driver, Otto, was

taking her to a dental appointment by way of the back roads, she noticed two ragamuffin boys walking toward the beach. They were carrying pails and home-made fishing poles. Otto slowed the car and said, "Well, look at that, Mrs. Cooper. It's like something right out of the Tom Sawyer books."

Angel looked out and saw her grandson Pete looking right back in at her. Otto recognized the boys, too, and almost stopped the car, but when Angel saw the bare feet and the tattered shirts, she told him to drive on. She didn't want to be late at the dentist's office. They already had enough to talk about.

For the next five minutes or so, Angel shook her head a lot. What had she done to deserve such a daughter? Sometimes she regretted having sent Priscilla to college, and she wondered if any other mothers felt the same way. She even thought of writing the college president to complain about what they were doing to the nation's young women. Once she asked her sister, Lavinia, who lived in Savannah, if it was possible for a sweet young thing like Priscilla to major in mortification.

"Whatever do you mean?" Lavinia asked, and Angel proceeded to give her an example of exactly the sort of thing she meant.

"Why, dear sister, have you forgotten the day you and I went with Priscilla to tea at the Huguenot church? Priscilla was probably a college sophomore at the time, and someone visiting from Philadelphia – up where wit is a rare commodity – came over and asked, 'What do the three rivers down here in Charleston make?' Well, Lavinia, we all know perfectly well what they make, and so does Priscilla. But no, the girl could not simply ignore the question, no, she could not, she had to go on, like a dog with a bone, and say, 'No, madame, I do not know what the three rivers coming together here in Charleston make.' And then she had the effrontery to ask this perfect stranger, 'Is it a puddle?' Lavinia, you remember that. Don't try to fob me off by saying you don't."

"Yes, dear Angel," said Lavinia, "I do remember that," and then she laughed her Lavinia laugh. "And I also remember how you leaned over and whispered in my ear that you hoped they did not make that puddle in the middle of your Tillie's newly mopped floor."

"Oh, yes, Lavinia, I had forgotten that part about the floor. Why is it you always have to remind me of things I would rather forget? You are no help at all for these wrinkles of mine."

No, as far as Angel was concerned, 1965 was the beginning of the end.

* * * * * * * *

"Wasn't that your grandmother?" Tim asked as he and Pete continued on the way to their favorite fishing spot. Little did they know that, before the day was over, they would see another lady wearing pearls and riding in a fancy car.

This happened later that afternoon at Briar's Corner Store,

not far from the beach. Pete and Tim were scrutinizing the goods available at their favorite hangout. Pete's mother, Priscilla, called Mr. Briar's store the Carolina seacoast's chief source of slivers, and every day when they returned home, she asked, "Do I need to fetch my needle and check the soles of your feet?"

As the boys were examining the gumballs, they saw a man and a woman, dressed in what looked like matching seersucker suits, watching their every move. Pete and Tim checked for a car outside, saw one from Florida, and decided to put on a show for the visitors.

They switched into their ambling act. After this they hitched up their trousers which were, like the shirts on their backs, raggedy. They stuck their thumbs in their pants pockets, and just when they knew they were being observed again, they added a bit of strut to their swagger and heard what they always heard when "the fish began to fry." Mr. Briar laughed. Having received that confirmation, they knew they were on a roll. It was time to bring out the southern drawl starring their best versions of the "ain'ts" and the "you alls."

When they finished with that, they paused and waited for the "wells" and the "I nevers." Once they were in receipt of these encomiums, they looked at the candy display, and Tim said, "Well, little Peteyman, I ain't never, not in all my born days, seen anything as pretty as this little purple gumball. Too bad we ain't got even a plugged nickel between us. Now ain't that a cryin' shame?"

That always did the trick. The seersucker lady turned to Mr. Briar, pressed some small change into his cupped hand, and asked him to tell the boys she wanted to make them a present of two purple gumballs.

With bright shining faces – and maybe just a touch of smudge – the two boys thanked their benefactress "in just the sweetest way possible." Then, with a rush, Tim began to limp. The gentleman in the matching seersucker asked if the boy were in pain. Pete answered that Tim had just run a splinter the size of a small railroad tie through his toe. Very adroitly, Pete reached down, found it, and held it up for all to see. That sliver brought with it a pair of new shoes for each of the boys, as well as shirts, together with several bars of Lava soap.

The last act was inevitable. Even with new shoes, it was obviously painful for Tim to walk, what with the wound and all still hurting so much. A ride home in the deluxe automobile was quickly offered and just as quickly accepted by the two boys whose nicknames were "dispatch" and "alacrity." The two of them waved to Mr. Briar as the car drove away.

Their new friends asked directions and turned the car toward the beach, but Pete thumped on the sumptuous cushions, stopped the driver in time, and said, "No, no, my house is in the other direction, go out to the highway."

The car turned almost all the way around, headed for the cypresses, and ended up in low meadow country, where there were white board fences and barns with cupolas. This was not exactly what the car's owners had been expecting, but they weren't yet at the point where questions needed to be asked.

That happened a short time later when Pete thumped again and pointed to a gate that opened on to a side road. The sound of the car echoed through a grove of oak trees, and then the boys said, "There, beyond the rock wall, that's where Pete lives."

As the car approached the house, their new friends asked the boys if they wanted to be taken around to the back, but both boys said, "No, everybody uses the front door." The car rolled to a stop. Pete's mother and her friends got up from chaises and lawn chairs and crossed the terrace to greet the new arrivals. Both boys stepped out of the car. Pete introduced his mother and told her about the adventure they had had while Tim showed her the presents they had received.

Priscilla invited her new guests to get out of the car and join the party for a splash of something refreshing, but the startled strangers begged off and said they needed to continue on their way. They asked Tim if they could deliver him to his home, and Tim, not forgetting his drawl, said, "No, I'm not from around here. I'm just visiting my friend Pete for the week. My family lives up in Columbia. My daddy's the governor."

Plaza Hotel, New York City

Berlin ist eine Reise Wert
(Berlin is worth a trip)

I.   New York

In 1995 college friends offered me the use of their Manhattan apartment for a month while they visited their son and his family in San Francisco. Before leaving, they introduced me to their neighbor, Lois. A week later this young woman invited me to meet her parents for lunch at a nearby restaurant. That's how I met Mr. and Mrs. Nichols, investors in Broadway plays. Lois and her parents had recently returned from Europe. I asked them about the trip, and they told me all about it. Later, when lunch was over, Mrs. N. said the afternoon had flown by; then she turned to her husband and added, "Just like the horses at Belmont."

* * * * * * *

At first, Mrs. N. did not think the trip to Germany was a good idea, but to keep peace in the family, she decided to go to Berlin with her husband, Joe.

"We'll be back in New York by October," Joe said, because he knew that month was her favorite time of year in the city.

* * * * * * * *

Their daughter, Lois, had always been grateful to her parents for choosing a hospital on Fifth Avenue for her birth because that decision resulted in the family moving to East 79th Street before she learned to walk. From the time she was small, she wanted to spend her every waking moment in Central Park. Lois liked to tell people the park was like a third parent to her, and one of the reasons she liked to pass the time there was because, when her father was at home, her parents engaged in an epic battle that was as close to knock-down, drag-out as propriety permits.

Once, during a radio interview, Mrs. Billy Graham was asked if at any time during her long marriage she had ever thought of divorce. Ruth Graham replied, "Divorce, never; murder, yes." After hearing that, Mrs. N. went out, bought a dish towel, cross-stitched it with the words "Divorce, never; murder, yes," then framed it herself and hung it on the bedroom wall where their wedding picture had been.

Joe, Lois's father, never one to be outdone by the "little woman," liked to show the towel to visitors, and at some point in the conversation he always said, "You know, I'm grateful to my wife for giving me a reason to live." Someone would always ask, "Oh, yes, Joe, and what is that reason?" Joe would gleefully reply, "I want to live because my wife wants me dead." Then he would smile at Mrs. N., she would return his gaze, and they would laugh a little laugh

194

together.

That's about the only laughter there was in that family when Lois was growing up. Later on, things improved a bit. Lois thought her father had a mistress, and after that woman died in a horseback-riding accident, Mrs. N. mellowed a little. The Berlin trip may have been an attempt on Joe's part to bring them closer together. Lois thought his plan had worked, and every time she visited, she looked in the bedroom to see if her mother had taken down the cross-stitching, but she never did.

* * * * * * * *

Joe told Mrs. N. that an administrative department in the Berlin city government had commissioned a list of prominent New Yorkers and was planning to invite them to visit Germany. The Nichols family was on the list. Mrs. N. asked if this invitation had anything at all to do with the New York-Berlin sister city program. Joe said he wasn't sure about that, maybe it did, maybe it did not, but, in any case, the trip was free: taxi fare to and from the New York airport, first-class airfare across the Atlantic and back, limo provided in Berlin, plus connecting double bedrooms (Lois was also invited) in a top-starred hotel with views of the Tiergarten, the Brandenburg Gate, and the American Embassy.

"We'd be foolish to pass up an offer as good as this one," Joe added, and Mrs. N. had already reached the same conclusion. It was to be a trip filled with lots of activities: sight-seeing, meetings with important players on Berlin's cultural scene, dinners, concerts, as well as a tour of the Royal Prussian porcelain factory.

"Will there be any theater visits?" Mrs. N. had asked. "That, too," Joe answered, "the whole nine yards."

When Mrs. N. saw the names of those who would be making the trip with them, she was impressed. The list included people from different walks of life, and several names on it were Jewish, like theirs. Lois and her parents began looking forward to traveling together; they went out and bought expensive luggage. It was fun, and heaven knows the family had never had much of that.

Brandenburg Gate, Berlin

Marlene Dietrich

Paris Tribute

II.   Berlin

Berlin, like New York, has been an international destination for most of its history. People said it had more Chinese restaurants than any other city outside China, but Joe said every city on the planet could probably come up with claims like that, so he advised Mrs. N. to keep a salt shaker handy.

Unlike New York, Berlin is not a city of tall buildings, but in many other respects, the two cities are much alike. "Who needs tall buildings anyway," Mrs. N. had asked, "when they're filled mostly with people who aren't there?" Joe and Lois looked at each other – and then at the floor – but Mrs. N. didn't seem to notice.

At first glance the people one sees on the streets of Berlin look much like Americans from all over, but appearances can of course be deceiving. It's the way Berliners interact with one another that puts them on a par with New Yorkers. The natives of both cities can be brash and rude – in your face in a flash – but they leave you alone if you don't bother them. In both cities, however, visitors are often surprised by how quick people are to help when an emergency situation presents itself.

* * * * * * * *

Toward the end of her life, Marlene Dietrich lived first in New York City – where her name was in the Manhattan telephone directory – and then in Paris, on the Avenue Montaigne, across the Seine River from the Eiffel Tower. After Dietrich's death, Germans were surprised to learn she had made arrangements to be buried in Berlin.

It had taken a while for them to forget the pictures of Dietrich surrounded by American GIs at USO shows during the war. They had faulted Dietrich for having gone to America and called her an opportunist. But as time passed, they remembered that opportunism was a home-grown product, a characteristic she had no doubt learned from them, and they stifled themselves. It took time, but they made their peace with her.

Eventually, Dietrich returned to Berlin and sang for them, but before she made public appearances, she visited the city incognito. Her mother lived there.

Dietrich considered herself to be a Berliner at heart, and she regarded Berlin both as her home and as a place apart. She said Berlin was not like the rest of Germany, that it was like New York, that it existed in a realm of its own making, one that transcended national boundaries. It was in Germany, certainly, but it was not of Germany. It was German, but it was much more than that, perhaps because Berlin, like New York, was shaped by immigrants. For example, after the Edict of Nantes was revoked by Louis XIV of France in 1685, many Jews from Vienna and tens of thousands of Huguenots from France migrated to Berlin in order to escape persecution. Whatever the reason may be, when it comes to New York and Berlin, visitors agree that smart-aleck, wise-cracking, and acerbic wit are qualities that characterize both populations.

Edict of Nantes, 1598

* * * * * * * *

Expectation sat in the airplane as the New Yorkers drew closer to Berlin, and those who ended up in the limo with the Nichols family did not have long to wait for their first encounter with Berlin's wry sense of humor.

Berlin's streets are busy, and being stuck in traffic is not uncommon. As the chauffeur ably dealt with its frustrations, he had to stop for a red light. There was just one car in front of the limo. The New Yorkers had to wait for a long time. When the light did change, the car in front of them did not move an inch, not even a centimeter, even though its driver seemed to be awake and paying attention. So, they had to wait some more. Although there were vehicles to the right, left, and rear of the limo, not a single horn was heard. It was as though time had gone on break. Finally, all patience seemed exhausted, and tempers were fraying when the limo driver leaned forward and said to no one in particular, "You might as well move it, buddy. That light ain't gonna get any greener."

In his American blue jeans, the driver had shown himself to be as quick on the draw as any fellow out by the corral in the Old West. People in the limo smiled; some of them laughed out loud and then, from the back of the car, Lois heard a familiar voice say, "Did we bring him with us all the way from New York?"

It was Mrs. N. Lois waited for her father's riposte, but it didn't come until after dinner that evening, and by then it was too late. The game was over. The score was 1 for Mrs. Nichols, 0 for her husband.

Welcome to Berlin.

The French Cathedral, Berlin

Courtesy Peter J. O'Toole

*Once Upon a Time

The Kapellmeister

Once upon a time,[*] far away and long ago, there were two brothers, twins. They had seven younger brothers and sisters. Their parents were dead. One of the twins played the piano. He taught the younger children how to play the piano, and he encouraged them to learn a musical instrument in school. The other twin did not know how to play the piano and said it was a waste of time to practice. It made him angry when his brother and one or another of the children made music together. It irritated him just to see someone sit down at the piano. He was jealous of his brother, and, as Shakespeare tells us, jealousy is a destructive force. Whenever the unhappy brother heard the piano, he would go downstairs to his wood shop, slam the door, and begin making a terrible din with his hammer and saw. Sometimes the family could hear him muttering to himself, asking how is this going to put bread on the table? He scoffed at his brother, called him crazy and stupid, and said he should do something useful instead of playing the same old scales day after day.

* * * * * * * *

---

[*] Please note that this story begins and ends as fairy tales do, but it is not a fairy tale.

One day the village choirmaster was walking past the house. The windows were open, and he heard a piano and a clarinet. He stopped to listen. When the music was over, he applauded and said the piece they had played was beautiful.

"I'm having a concert at my house next month for some friends," he said. "I would be pleased if the two of you could join us. Some of the guests will be playing music I have selected for them. I have a piece with me now that I would like you to play. It's a clarinet sonata by Johannes Brahms."

The piano part of the sonata was more difficult than anything the musical brother was accustomed to playing. He knew he would have to practice a lot if he wanted to avoid making a fool of himself. As soon as the choirmaster was out of sight and hearing range, he sat down and began working on it.

Right away the jealous brother heard him. He stormed into the music room, still carrying the hammer and saw. He hated hearing the music start up again. He interrupted it and asked, "Must we always have such a racket going on in here? Can't we ever have some peace and quiet in this house?"

* * * * * * * *

The next week the choirmaster happened to walk past the house a second time. The windows were open, as before. He heard the piano and the clarinet, but he also heard the hammering and the sawing. Again, he waited for the players to finish, and when they did, he invited them to practice at the church.

"It's quiet there," he said, "away from the noise you have here at home."

At that very moment, just in time to hear this remark, the noisy brother appeared on the stairs. He was angrier than ever, but he said nothing. The choirmaster continued, "I am honored to count the castle Kapellmeister among my friends. He will be joining our little group next month." The noisy brother knew who the Kapellmeister was. He went back into the shop and sullenly resumed his hammering.

As soon as the choirmaster was gone, the by-now furious brother reappeared. "You are even more full of yourself than I thought possible," he said. "If you really think that someone like the Kapellmeister wants to listen to the likes of you, well, all I can say is that you should have your head examined, and your hind quarters as well."

He went on and on, making a scene, berating his brother with such nastiness that, finally, the musical brother said he would not play at the concert. When the jealous brother heard this, he smiled his crooked smile.

The musical brother told the children he could not play, the piece was too difficult, and he did not have enough time to practice. His little sister, however, continued to practice the clarinet part at school. She was too young to understand what was happening between her brothers.

The family went to the concert, but the musical brother told his sister again that he had decided not to play. He did not want to embarrass himself. The Kapellmeister appeared and told the musical brother he was looking forward to hearing the Brahms sonata.

When the musical brother declined, saying he had not had enough time to practice, the other brother broke in and said, just as sweet as pie, "Oh, he's just being modest, and it's a false modesty. What he wants is for you to entreat him; he likes it when people do that. Actually, he's been practicing the whole month long. The house has been filled with the sound of music. He's been practicing so much I thought it would set the piano on fire." This comment was followed by an audible chuckle.

The musical brother regarded it as unseemly to be seen in direct confrontation with his brother, so he relented, but he knew the sonata would not go well.

When the concert was over, the Kapellmeister spoke to the untruthful brother and said, "I did not know your brother played the piano." The resentful brother responded, "Oh, yes, he does, but he's not very good at it, as you can tell from what you've just heard. If I spent half as much time at the piano as he does, I would be able to play far better." The Kapellmeister was not surprised by this remark; he was a good judge of character, and he recognized mean-spiritedness when he saw it.

The musical brother overheard this conversation, but he

waited until it was over before showing himself. The Kapellmeister turned to him and said, "I can tell simply by your deft touch at the keyboard that you have a natural talent for the piano, a great gift. I want to invite you to begin music studies at the royal conservatory. It is clear to me that your situation is not easy, but it is equally plain that you have succeeded against formidable odds and have persevered in spite of the many obstacles thrown in your way. You have continued to work and to apply yourself diligently even though your family has been touched by tragedy. It is to these efforts that you owe your success. You deserve a place at the conservatory."

The angry brother was so enraged by this that he could not see straight. His face turned as red as the proverbial beet in August. Onlookers feared he had blown a gasket. His eyes bulged out; then they crossed and looked at each other over the bridge of his regrettable nose. And if the bitter brother has not had the wit to stanch his jealousy by now, then his eyes are still crossed, so that he sees very little – and understands less – to this very day.

Bayreuth Opera House

Americans in Germany

Between Bayreuth, Germany, where Richard Wagner built his famous opera house, and the Czech border, you'll find the Fichtelgebirge, so named for its evergreen trees and the terrain. Although its higher elevations are less than half of what one finds in the Black Hills of South Dakota, the waters from the Fichtelgebirge flow north to the North Sea; south into the Danube; east toward Prague, and west into the River Main, which eventually joins the Rhine.

When Germany was divided at the end of World War II, the Fichtelgebirge found itself in American hands. It is a picturesque part of Germany, and the Americans liked it. Many West Berliners liked it, too, and they escaped the restrictions of their city by buying or renting vacation homes there. It was relatively easy to reach by car, even though the East German roads were not in good repair, and drivers had to be on the alert for speed traps.

In 1983 a West Berlin family invited us to visit them in the Fichtelgebirge. We drove there from Vienna. The Berliners were restoring an old farmhouse in a village not far from the point where East Germany, West Germany, and the Czech Republic met. It was the kind of house where one almost has to assume a kneeling position in order to pass from one room to the next. It was either bend low or run the risk of banging one's forehead on the lintel. One smack on the forehead and you'd remember to stoop from then on. Raising a lintel is expensive, and it can weaken the structure if it is not done well. It also compromises the integrity of the building, something many architects are reluctant to do.

The role of the forests in German lore is legendary. Today the forests are protected for many reasons: economic, environmental, recreational, and as a food source. One doesn't have to stay near a forest for very long before being invited on an expedition looking for mushrooms. Like the morel mushrooms in Minnesota and across the northern states, the chanterelle mushrooms (*Pfifferlinge*) in Germany are prized for their refined flavor. Family outings are often planned around them, and gathering mushrooms is a cherished tradition.

Getting to know the village locals is also part of vacationing in the country. It's easy to do. Stop in at a barn, or go to the local pub. Chances are the first time an outsider sets foot in the pub people will turn their heads to look, but after that, even if you're American – as we are – they will likely ignore you. Later, however, they'll take the time to get better acquainted. Europeans are generally more reserved than Americans; most of them won't stay too long, or intrude overmuch on your privacy. It's up to you.

* * * * * * * *

We had only been in the village a few days when we heard concerns expressed about military operations in the area. The village was near East Germany, so one saw signs of U.S. forces here more often than in places farther away from the border.

One day while the grown-ups were sitting in the garden and our children were playing in the park with the village children, we heard whooping and hollering followed by the rumble of heavy military equipment. I went out to see what was happening. The children were running down to the village crossing. A line of American tanks was coming down the slope. The soldiers were at their stations on the armored personnel carriers, holding their weapons. Some of the soldiers were white like me; many were not. I was moved by this scene of what America stands for, but then I heard the children making a lot of noise at the corner. At first they seemed to be greeting the troops in friendly fashion, but then I noticed that the clamor had an edge to it. I looked at the soldiers more carefully. They were stony-faced. None of them were waving to the youngsters. The children had not put on their happy faces for this event. They were not waving their fists, but their gestures were not forbearing or thoughtful, and the noise was upsetting. My general impression was that the men in the tanks were not being made to feel welcome. I looked for my children and saw them not far away. At that moment, they turned and saw me, too. Clearly, they were not enjoying this meeting between the American soldiers and the local children. They looked wan and crestfallen. I wanted to get them out of there.

As my children turned away from the group and began walking toward me, I knew they were feeling something of what it means to be part of the "other," of not quite belonging. Although they spoke and understood German and had friends here, they knew this was not their home. Home was somewhere else, a place on the other side of a great divide. We were American, like the men in the tanks, and nothing could change that.

At dinner that evening we were told that the tanks were disliked because they made marks in the smooth asphalt road surface. I recalled seeing the tanks turn the corner. Tanks cannot turn corners smoothly, as cars and trucks do. No, they turn in jerks, stopping, turning, going forward and back, and then repeating it all over again. And, yes, the lugs were leaving marks on the road. There's not a lot a tank can do to avoid making scars in asphalt on a summer day. It's a fact of life, something that happens from time to time, like war.

Lugs on U. S. Military Vehicle

Rex Harrison

Henry Higgins

Like many Southerners, Dr. Reyn Carter spent the summers in the mountain state of Colorado. In 1958, he taught Southern history at the University of Colorado in Boulder. In his class it became apparent that all southern accents are not alike.

Dr. Carter spoke with a soft southern accent. During the first week of classes, a young man from the South stood up and asked Dr. Carter a question, "Why is it," he said, "that every time I say something up here in the North everyone starts to laugh?"

For just a second there was silence in the room, and then the laughter started. Dr. Carter was taken aback, but then the hint of a smile appeared on his face, and he raised his hand to cover it, as if he had been about to sneeze. By that time, the room was filled with raucous laughter.

Dr. Carter, calling on the grace that is proverbial in the American South, looked down at the floor, deepened his own drawl and replied, "Sometimes, when we Southerners come up north, we find ourselves obliged to adjust the cut of our tailoring to match the style that prevails in this part of the country.* Don't worry, you'll

---

* Lillian Hellman in the 1950s refused to name names for the House Committee on Un-American Activities. She said, "I cannot and will not cut my conscience to fit this year's fashions." (Letter to HUAC, May 19, 1952)

get used to it, and so will those who hear you." Dr. Carter was a retired Foreign Service officer. His cool response showed that his diplomatic skills had not gone rusty. Without further comment, the class went back to work.

One hears of people in Europe having such strong accents, while speaking their native languages, that their compatriots make fun of them. It is said that children in schoolyards can be especially merciless, but this was the first time I had experienced such a thing for myself.

* * * * * * * *

I lived in the Language House on the CU campus in Boulder during the summer of 1958. One of the French tutors, Renée B., was a Fulbright exchange student from France. We were in the same art history class. She was trying to improve her English, and I was interested in French architecture. On the way to class one afternoon, she invited me to join her grammar study group, and I accepted. She taught the class in English so that anyone with an interest in grammar could take part, and the group met three evenings a week at a wine bar near the campus.

At break-time one evening, a language house resident asked if Renée would help him with French pronunciation. She told him his accent was fine, and added that many French adolescents would be happy to be able to pronounce French as well as he did. End of conversation.

* * * * * * * *

At the end of the summer my half-brother, Cary, came out to Colorado to hike. With Renée and me, he joined a mountaineering club, and we spent a month above timberline. Cary already had his degree in architecture and French. At the end of September, he and Renée returned to France, where he found a job with an architectural firm in Paris.

They were married at Christmas time. I went to Paris for the wedding and found that Cary was often introduced as the American who spoke French so well that everyone said he should be on stage at the Comédie Française.

A year later I graduated, found a teaching job in Minnesota, and from then on spent my summers in France. As the years went by, my French gradually improved.

Renée's brother, his wife, and their three children had a vacation home in Burgundy. Every summer they invited Renée, Cary, and me to spend some time with them in the vineyard country south of Dijon. Renée's sister-in-law did not care to speak English, so she and Renée spoke French together.

In Colorado and in France Renée had usually spoken English with me, while I spoke French. This was the first time I heard her speak French in a sustained conversation. I noticed that something in her French had changed since our days in Boulder. I asked myself what had happened, and my question was answered a few days later.

We often ate lunch at Chez Paul in Gevrey-Chambertin. When the weather was nice, we gathered on the terrace and wondered if it was Switzerland we could see in the eastern distance.

One day a Parisian couple asked to join us. They introduced themselves: Madame and Monsieur Frommer. He was the chief of police in a suburb west of Paris. He spoke English, but his wife did not, so out of courtesy to her, we switched to French.

It was an agreeable group, and we soon found ourselves spending time together almost every day. The police chief was a devotee of American and English musicals. His favorite was "My Fair Lady;" he knew all the songs by heart. He was an admirer of Henry Higgins (played by Rex Harrison in the 1964 film), and, like Mr. Higgins, Mr. Frommer enjoyed the challenge of trying to determine where people came from, based on their accents. He told me he had been trying to place my accent. He said he knew I was French, but he could not say just where in France I had been born and raised. No one in the group offered to help him. Then he turned to Renée and said her accent presented no problem at all because he knew she was, without a doubt, Swedish.

Renée's brother spoke up and said, "Well, that's because my sister managed to change her unfortunate accent while she was in America. Remember, Renée, how we used to tease you when we were children? We all laughed and laughed when you started talking like the mother and daughter who moved to our town from a province that shall forever remain nameless. You and Anne were in the same class; you practically lived at their house during all your years in grade school."

My brother Cary and I looked at each other in amazement. It was as if the earth had moved beneath our feet. To say that Renée was incensed on hearing this from her brother is to understate the seriousness of the situation.

Renée was livid. When her brother used the word "unfortunate," I saw her kick him hard in the shins. His knee jerked upward, causing the glass-topped table to tip. In that instant, time seemed to slip into slow motion. The glass cracked into multiple pieces which fell to the tile floor and shattered.

Without a word, Renée stood up and left the terrace. I realized in that long, drawn-out moment how painful a subject her unattractive accent was for her, and that I had been right to think her French had changed. She no longer carried strong traces of the accent of the family that had moved West to her birthplace, but she had also lost something of her native tongue. What Mr. Frommer had said was true. She now spoke French with a Swedish accent.

Later that same afternoon, through the curtained glass doors between our rooms, I heard Renée say to Cary that Frommer was a pompous twit and that it was her devout wish never to lay eyes on him or his frumpy wife again.

Her wish was granted. The next day reception told us the

Frommers had an emergency at home and had taken an early train back to Paris.

Vineyard

Gevrey-Chambertin

Stop Right There!

It is not uncommon for English-speaking people to be overwhelmed when visiting foreign places. Someone should write a book on how to survive in a country where the first language is not English. If you plan to write such a book, here is a tip you might want to consider. It can be useful when speaking with certain Europeans in railroad stations, restaurants, hotels, and even on the telephone.

Let's begin at the main railway station in Munich, Germany. It's seven o'clock in the morning. Our train leaves in an hour. We have missed breakfast at the hotel. We are hungry, and the restaurants in the station are not yet open, so we have to find something to eat at one of those small, kiosk-like places. We have looked and looked, but all we have seen so far are those big salty pretzels whose circular lines remind us of the logos one sees on some Japanese cars.

Finally, we find a shop that has yogurt in its showcase. That would be perfect. The only problem is we do not have a spoon; however, at that very moment we see a shiny tin pail filled to overflowing with white plastic spoons.

The "growler" who lives in my stomach is noisily making his bed, and I ask him if yogurt will be OK. He says yogurt will be fine. I try to catch the clerk's attention, but it won't be easy because dozens of people are standing in line, or what passes for a line in many places on the continent, including France and Germany. Somehow I have to get closer to the counter. After several attempts, I succeed. Now I see why people are bumping into one another. There is only one person working behind the counter, and he looks as if he has not had a wink of sleep since the dawn's early light last graced Baltimore.

The French and Germans are equally good at making apple cake, but they are equally bad when it comes to lining up, something the English have always seemed able to do with the greatest of ease. It may be that learning how to spell the words "queue," and "queuing" has taken the fight out of them.

The server looks at me. I look at him. He says a German word, and I know what it means, so I say, "May I have a cup of that yogurt over there, please?" In the quickest move I've seen him make at any time during the past half hour, he places a yogurt in front of me. It happens to be green, something that, understandably, seems to have escaped the eye of the growler, so *tant pis* for him. Then I ask, again in German, "And may I have one of those white plastic spoons with which to eat it?" At the mention of white plastic spoons, the server's mood changes markedly. One would think I had asked for the moon and some stars to go with it. His face becomes contorted, giving the impression that he's trying to control two sentences that are locked in mortal combat while trying to exit his mouth at the same time. The one party seems to have gathered its forces in the left cheek, while the other has marshaled its verbiage on the right side.

The forces on the left win out for the moment. The server lets me know that racist comments of the kind I have just uttered are illegal in Germany, and then asks if I think for even a moment that just because I am white, he is going to skip around and sing a song? I have no idea what he's talking about.

That this outburst from the left is uncalled for goes without saying. It is, in a word, outrageous, and anyone who has the audacity to mouth such nonsense should be thoroughly thrashed and throttled without a moment's delay, giving no thought to the morrow, and letting the devil take the hindmost.

But, in the interest of world harmony, I decide to let this pass. I hold my tongue, which is rather hard to do because I am neither a dentist nor a doctor. While I'm making this effort, the clerk's right cheek gets its act together and lets fly with "What the bloody buck do you think this establishment is, a hotel?" I look around to see if a pillow or some other accoutrement usually associated with a hotel has attached itself to me, but no, that's not the case. The case is that this remark – or so it seems to me – is not only totally unnecessary, it is also pure, unmitigated guff.

It is time to share the tip I promised you at the beginning of this story.

With the measured power of a locomotive that has been gathering steam all the way from the northern plains down to Chicago, I say, quite simply, but with incontrovertible emphasis, "Stop right there! We find ourselves today in one of the great train stations of the world with a group of people who would like nothing more than to eat some yogurt, but due to some misfiring quirk in the circumlocutory rhythms of the universe – or because we were not fortunate enough to have been born with a white plastic spoon in our mouth – we find ourselves without a spoon to eat with. So, we are asking you again, and in your own language, to please provide us with one of those white plastic spoons, of which you possess a bountiful supply in that container over there on that shelf right behind you. Please do not deny your fellow creatures the advantage of eating yogurt with a spoon rather than a toothbrush. Hand over one of those spoons right now, and make it snappy."

Believe me, after all this, chances are pretty good he will give you a spoon, and you'll be out of there in plenty of time to catch your train, where you will be able to sit down and eat your yogurt in something approaching perfect and sublime tranquility, unless, of course, you are traveling second class, the train is full, and you have to stand all the way to Stuttgart.

Mercedes Benz Logo

Courtesy Lisa Abascal Larson

Princeton Gate

The Rest is Silence

I.   Manahawkin, New Jersey

If it's as far to Tipperary as it is from Princeton to Manahawkin, it's a long way. And if it's raining the whole time, it's really too far to go for a cup of tea, even if the tea is as tasty as what your grandmother used to make. But sometimes the fates conspire against us, and we find ourselves doing things we would never have considered even if the weather had been nice and we had been closer to home.

It was the summer of 1991, and my trip to Boston was going to be almost 100 miles longer because I had decided to visit my cousin Elisabeth and her family on the Jersey shore.

It was just after three o'clock in the afternoon when I pulled up in front of their large white house. I was running late, and it was still raining. Elisabeth saw the car come in, walked the few steps from the veranda to the passenger door, and handed me an umbrella.

"You're just in time for tea," she said, and hurried back to the house.

I followed her inside and saw that the rooms were beautifully furnished. Elisabeth had married into a family that owned a string of furniture stores that ran from Manahawkin to Florida. The kitchen table was set for tea, and the garden outside looked like something from Winterthur in nearby Delaware. Brick paths and a white picket fence kept white and yellow irises from taking over the space nearest the house. Apparently, our grandfather's town garden had made an impression on Elisabeth, too. Her husband, son, and a daughter came to greet me. Another daughter was at work. The tea was the best I'd had since our grandmother's day, and I said so. Elisabeth smiled and did not deny it. There were sugar cookies to go with the tea. Lovely.

They knew I couldn't stay long, so we began working out the best way to get me from New Jersey to Massachusetts. The George Washington Bridge was probably as good a route as any. Elisabeth's son made a map that showed the way from the bridge to White Plains and into Connecticut. He knew all the highway names and numbers because his fiancée lived in White Plains.

When he finished with the directions, we turned to the weather. They all agreed it had been bad for weeks. I knew that already, because earlier that summer my daughter had a difficult time driving from Vermont to Cape Cod. That storm was so bad that people began comparing it to the hurricane of 1938. I had heard about that storm, too, because our neighbor lady, originally from Boston, and her family had lived through it, though just barely. I hoped the weather would improve as I drove north.

Then it was time to get underway. Elisabeth and her family thanked me for visiting and packed more sugar cookies in my Gokey's bag.

Courtesy Lakewood Cemetery, Minneapolis

Ronald A. Gjenne Jr., President

George Washington Bridge, Hudson River

II.   Radio Show

On the way from Manahawkin to the George Washington Bridge, there were signs for towns whose names I remembered from my sixth-grade geography book, Elizabeth among them. Soon the bridge towers loomed in the distance, and I felt almost at home. I had crossed that bridge many times. It was still raining, but the rental car's windshield wipers were efficient and easy to operate. The trip was going well.

But then, not long after crossing the East River, I lost my way. I exited the highway, stopped in a parking lot at a fast food place, and was ready to go in to ask directions when a group of young people began moving my way. They looked menacing, as if they were approaching with intent. I decided to get out of there.

By this time it was dark, raining hard, and I was lost. Whenever there was a sign that looked trustworthy and pointed north, I followed it, meandering around in a part of the country that was heavily industrial, and that was stressful for me.

There were fearsome flashes of lightning every once in a while, and these were followed by incredible claps of thunder that seemed so close I thought the car's motor was giving up the ghost just a few feet in front of me.

One station on the car radio didn't have too much static, and it was broadcasting a call-in program. There was a host, and, little by little, I learned that the topic being discussed that evening was the

Great Hurricane of 1938. I began paying more attention to bridges and overpasses and noticed that some of them passed over water. When there was lightning, I caught glimpses of whitecaps that looked mean and angry.

A man who called in to the radio station had a lot to say about the 1938 storm, and he was saying it well. Like me, he was in his car. I listened intently, even though the crackling reception was making that difficult. The caller's family had a house on the Connecticut shore in the 1930s. I wondered if I was getting close to it.

Because of the pouring rain, traffic had slowed. Cars were passing me, but they weren't going too fast, and I began looking for a man in a late-model car who was talking on his cell phone.

The story was interesting and getting better all the time. It took my mind off my situation. Even though it would have been wiser to turn off the radio and concentrate on driving, I wasn't, for the moment at least, in any trouble. I continued listening and hoped to run out of the bad weather. The program host did not interrupt the caller often or ask him many questions. No doubt he recognized a good thing when he heard it. The caller was telling how he, his parents, and several siblings had been at their family's beach house that day in 1938:

> "The lights had gone out during the afternoon, but that had happened before, and the family enjoyed 'camping out' by candlelight. Later we realized we should have gone inland at that time. However, there

were plenty of candles and all of us, especially the younger children, liked crowding up against the big bulletproof windows in order to watch the lightning play on the water while the waves pounded the rocks along the shore.

"The wind was howling, and the house creaked, but that, too, was not unusual, and no one said they thought it was worse than other bad weather we and our grandparents had experienced over the years.

"Mother called us back to the kitchen for a cold supper. As we were passing through the living room with only candles to light the way, someone noticed there was water coming in under the front door, and it was rippling into the living room. By the time we reached the kitchen, our shoes had filled with water. Dad and Mother looked at each other and counted the children. Mother opened the door to the garage, led us out to the car, and helped us get in. No one thought of taking coats or jackets. I could hear Dad struggling with the garage door. When he managed to lift it, the water rushed in. I was afraid it would get in the car, but it didn't. Dad got himself into the car. Our parents called our names, and, in the dark, each one of us answered, five in the back seat, the youngest on Mother's lap in the front. Dad remembered that the car had headlights and turned them on. The car started. We backed out into the circle. Then Dad drove straight ahead, and we left the property by way of the service road, because it was higher. From there we drove out to the main road, which was also a causeway, and headed inland. We did not see any cars behind us, but looking through the trees coming up ahead of us we could see the flashing lights of the town's emergency vehicles. We rounded the bend in the road and saw more than a dozen police cars and fire trucks.

"A policeman put up his hand, and Dad stopped the car to talk with him. Other people came and spoke with Mother. They asked if we had seen any cars behind us, and we all answered we had not. Some of the emergency vehicles started down the road toward our house. We were told to go into town and then to continue inland."

* * * * * * * *

Just then the radio program host broke in and said, "Wow, that's quite a story," but the caller interrupted him and said, "Wait, wait, that's not all. It's not over yet, there's more."

The host did not try to stop him, and the caller continued:

"When Dad was allowed to return to our home site a few days later, he found that the wind and the water had moved our six-bedroom house off its foundations and carried it more than a hundred yards down the beach, where it lodged on the rocks and began breaking up in pieces. Apparently, the whole second story and roof were carried away, maybe out to sea. Nothing of the second floor or roof was ever found, not even a shingle.

"For years after that, every time Dad recounted what had happened to our house, he mentioned shingles. Whenever we went out there, I looked for shingles, hoping to find one for him. He loved that house. All his life he had gone there every year, and I thought a shingle would be some comfort to him, but none of us ever found one.

"The first floor was now just a big pile of broken-up wood, windows and doors. My older brother and I pulled boards and beams out of the debris. We pretended to be playing a giant game of 'pick up sticks,' and then one day, right in the middle of all this destruction, and apparently undamaged, ..."

* * * * * * *

At that moment I thought a particularly loud, fierce crack of thunder had smashed the roof of my rental car. I cringed, but, no, the roof was intact. Nothing else happened. The sound had come from the radio. A moment later the program host asked, "What was that?"

There was no answer, and then he said, "Hello, caller, are you still there? Hello?"

Again, no answer. The announcer paused and then continued, "Well, our guest was calling from his car. Maybe the antenna was struck by lightning, or...," and then he stopped.

Seconds later he continued, "Well, it looks as if we have lost contact with our caller. We'll have to go on without him. Let's continue with the next person waiting on the line. Are you there, next caller? Are you there?"

Radio Announcer

Shore House

Madeleines

Madeleines

Mother and Dad left Bemelmans Bar, climbed into a taxi, and headed for the Rainbow Room where they planned to go dancing for the first time in more than thirty years. They were on their second honeymoon. The trip to New York City was a gift from mother's sister, Lillie. It was 1978.

* * * * * * *

Twenty years later, Mother and I were having afternoon tea in the garden at the farm, reminiscing about that visit to Manhattan. Mother called our conversation a "remembrance of things past." We had heard that Marcel Proust's flood of memories had been released not by a madeleine, but rather by something like toast, but this did not bother us. People had also begun referring to his book as *In Search of Lost Time*, but we did not follow suit. We thought the new title was clumsy and unpoetic. Mother, who carried a copy of Shakespeare's sonnets with her wherever she went, felt certain that Proust would agree with us.

* * * * * * *

In the early 1990s, I had taken my time reading Proust's *Remembrance of Things Past* in English, and then I read two biographies of Proust, one by William C. Carter of Alabama, the other by Jean-Yves Tadié of the Sorbonne in Paris. I also took all the French language classes offered by the College of St. Catherine in St. Paul, Minnesota, where I lived at that time.

In the mid-1990s, I began making annual trips to France, always in October, when the weather was mild, close to perfect.

Madeleines had long been one of our favorite teatime treats, and as soon as I arrived in France, I continued my search for the definitive madeleine, something I had been doing sporadically for many years, but now I spoke some French.

A friend recommended a French tutor, and I enrolled at *L'Institut de Touraine* in the venerable city of Tours, located on the Loire River 140 miles southwest of Paris. It took less than an hour to get there by fast train (*TGV*) from the French capital.

* * * * * * *

TGV

244

The Hotel Musée served as my headquarters. It was two blocks from the Rue Nationale in the old part of Tours. Tours was bombed and burned for a week during World War II, so not everything in the old part of the city is old, but much of it – like the Place Plumereau – has been painstakingly restored.

During the first weeks in Tours, I never met a madeleine I didn't like, but as time passed, I learned that all madeleines are not alike. Far from it. These modest, light-brown cakes can be as different from one another as the apple pies found in display cases all across the United States. I learned to be selective.

I found the object of my quest at Amélie's patisserie in the Rue Colbert, the "restaurant street" of Tours.

During the relaxed autumn afternoons from the 1990s into the 2000s, Amélie's madeleines were a regular feature of afternoon tea. I learned to look for color, "crumble," and a hint of lemon when making my choices.

One can gain a good idea of what a madeleine will be like by taking a considered look at the color. If it is dark brown around the edges, it will more than likely be too hard, or crusty. If it is too light, the madeleine may be a bit mealy, damp, or underdone. When you break it in half, there won't be a little shower of powdered sugar and crumbs on your plate, so try to avoid the extremes of light and dark. Golden is good, but a light yellowy color is better.

Photos in some glossy cookbooks would have us believe that a madeleine has to be golden, but that can be a bit much. It's not appealing to bite into something that looks like gold leaf at Versailles. Seek out a subtle color that looks good enough to eat, and then, like Goldilocks, keep looking until you find a madeleine that's just right.

The last thing is the hint of lemon. The heavenly touch of lemon is crucial to the whole enterprise. Triumph crowns the efforts of those who master the art of grating just the right amount of lemon zest. Lemon juice cannot help you here. As with so many things done well in life, it takes time, patience, and practice for a chef to get it right, and a discerning public will take its business to those who excel at the task.

A good madeleine, like all good food, is gratifying, a thing of beauty and delight, like a good cup of tea or hot chocolate – both of which go well with madeleines.

A recipe book that includes madeleines in its index will help you get started, but don't forget that madeleines can be skittish. They need to be handled with care.

* * * * * * * *

Mother was a good cook. On the day the two of us were reminiscing about the visit to Manhattan, she decided it was time to try her hand at making madeleines. I was happy to help. The next morning we drove to St. Paul. The first thing we did was check the Japanese garden on the small terrace of my town house on Ramsey Hill.

That afternoon we went to the Williams-Sonoma store at the Mall of America and bought the more expensive of the two madeleine pans they had in stock. The famous pan with the shell forms in it is hard to resist. It invites one to take it home and put on an apron.

The next morning we left for the farm. We always took the Southwest diagonal (Highway 169) through the Minnesota River Valley and stopped for morning coffee at Gustavus Adolphus College in St. Peter. Its hilltop view of the broad Minnesota River Valley reminds me of the Loire Valley between Blois and Villandry. We were back home in time for lunch.

We tried making madeleines that afternoon, but the little cakes always stuck to the pan and broke up or tore every time we tried to lift them. Later that week I went back to Williams-Sonoma and bought the less expensive pan. Mother and I tried again. This time the madeleines did not stick. A little nudge and they almost jumped out of the pan. Success at last.

Sometimes madeleines have "bumps." I find them distracting. First, they mar the lovely shape of the madeleine; second, madeleines with bumps on them tend to roll around on the plate, and third, bumps make the madeleines look a little like a child's bathtub toy. Do what you can to avoid them.

Madeleines made at home are less likely to have bumps than those one finds in stores.

(c) Touroinissime

Poulenc Château

A Chance Encounter

I.   Francis Poulenc

In the mid-1990s a friend gave me a letter of introduction to Francis Poulenc's niece. I wrote to Madame S., and we arranged to meet at Poulenc's country home between Amboise and Tours in the Loire River valley. Unfortunately, Madame S. had a medical emergency the morning of our meeting and was taken to Paris by air ambulance. She left a note at the lodge saying she regretted having to upset our "careful planning" and expressed the hope that we would be able to meet at a later date.

The caretaker showed me the small château and the wine cellar carved into the limestone cliffs behind it. He invited me to tour the grounds, and then he had to leave for Rochecorbon. I saw the Noizay vineyard for which Madame S. had gained the coveted Vouvray designation, even though it was not, strictly speaking, in Vouvray.

When I returned to the rental car, it would not start. I had no phone with me, so I decided to walk back to town to call the rental agency in Amboise. There were several large houses along the road that led out to the highway. The last one had an intercom mounted on the wall next to the driveway gate. I pressed the button, stated my business, and received an answer in perfect Oxbridge English. The owner of the house introduced himself, invited me to visit, and the iron gate opened by remote control. I walked up the gravel driveway. Mr. and Mrs. Briest met me at the terrace.

They called their mechanic in Amboise, but the office was closed until two o'clock; it was now just past noon. "Good," they said, "we have more than an hour in which to get better acquainted." It turned out to be an extraordinary hour, and I felt the gratitude that only a woebegone stranger far away from home can feel.

* * * * * * * *

The Briests had two children, a son and a daughter, both married, and both living with their families in New York City. Neither one of them was interested in running the family business, a small publishing house in Paris.

A grandson visited France from time to time and showed some interest in the company, but he did not speak German. The Briests did much of their business in the German-speaking countries, and they thought it essential that its director should not only speak German, but should speak it well, just as they did. I could see they did not hold out much hope of this happening anytime soon. They were disappointed, but stoic.

The grandson's parents lived on West 72nd Street in

Manhattan, not far from the Dakota on Central Park West. I knew that part of the city. A friend of mine had lived on the Upper West Side for many years, and I often visited him there. Now he was retired and living in France.

"I have an American friend who lives in Sancerre," I said. "He's a polyglot and speaks German very well."

The Briests immediately expressed an interest in meeting him. I telephoned Bob and reached him at his apartment in Paris. When I told him where I was, he asked to speak with my hosts. A few minutes later, they returned and said, "Everything is arranged. We are meeting him for lunch in Orléans on Wednesday."

Zabar's, New York City

* * * * * * *

A year later I was in Paris, and the Briests invited me to visit. They said their grandson Jeff would meet me at the *TGV* train station for Tours and would be wearing his grandfather's gardening hat. When I stepped off the train, there he was. He greeted me not in French or English, but in German, and he spoke it almost like a native.

"Your friend will be joining us for dinner," he said.

We went to the Château de Noizay restaurant. Bob arrived with the Briests.

"How did you teach this young man to speak excellent German in less than a year's time?" I asked.

The four of them told me they had drawn up a contract that stated exactly what was expected by both sides. Jeff had learned some German in high school, so he could read a little, but he could not write well. His grandparents said he would have their own business secretary to help him with writing, but speaking was another matter. They had told me the previous year that the boy could not communicate in a meaningful way in German, and when he tried, his accent was beyond abysmal.

The evening began and ended with champagne. No one mentioned what had been said the year before.

II.   Language Lessons

Bob told me they used the 1966 edition of the Heinz Griesbach and Dora Schulz textbook, *Deutsche Sprachlehre für Ausländer,*[*] together with its tapes – the same book the Goethe Institute uses at its cultural centers around the world.

Every other day for more than eight months, Jeff placed a conference call from New York City to Bob in Sancere. Mr. and Mrs. Briest listened in, but they never joined the conversation. At the beginning of every lesson, Bob turned on the story tape and paused it after every comma or break in the rhythm of the sentences, so Jeff could repeat. Bob corrected Jeff's pronunciation in a matter-of-fact way, and he never asked the young man to repeat anything a third time. They did this for an hour, every other day for two weeks, and at the end of that time, Jeff had to recite the story by heart. He also prepared a written exercise taken from the book for each phone session.

"Is that all there was to it?" I asked.

"Essentially, yes," Bob answered.

They did all fifteen chapters, two weeks per chapter. Jeff was encouraged to build his vocabulary in German, but how he did that was up to him.

There was one more important aspect to this work. At the end of each two-week period, Bob and Jeff stayed on the phone for a

_____

* Max Hueber Verlag, Munich

253

long, open-ended session. During this time Jeff kept his book closed, and Bob asked him several dozen questions, always in German, about the memorized story. Most, but not all, of the questions were in the teacher's manual. As you can imagine, Jeff had no trouble answering Bob's questions about the memorized story. The real test came when Bob asked Jeff to use imagination in answering the questions.

For example, one of the first stories included the sentence, "The map hangs in the back of the room." When Bob asked, "What hangs in the back of the room?" it was easy for Jeff to say, "The map hangs in the back of the room." But when Bob asked Jeff to make up his own answers to this question, Jeff had to stop for a minute to consider just how to do this. Bob knew his student was catching on when Jeff said, "The teacher hangs in the back of the room," and he followed this by naming all the other things he could think of that one might find hanging in the back of a room.

From that moment on, the classes were flying! The time on the phone was almost riotous. Jeff's grandparents, both of whom had grown up speaking French and German, could hardly believe their ears. In just a few weeks, Jeff was able to start speaking German with them, and after that it just got better and better. By the time they finished the fifteen chapters, Jeff could speak German, and his accent was remarkably good.

It was a pleasure to introduce Bob to the Briests, and they thanked me for bringing them together. It was an exuberant group that left the restaurant that evening.

* * * * * * * *

Here's how to do this for yourself: first, you have to find a teacher with a good accent, and that is not easy to do. Second, I have tried this technique with other textbooks, but I can assure you the magic resides with Griesbach and Schulz. Together, they produced a brilliant textbook. For outstanding results, it is crucial that students memorize the stories. Being able to read them well is not enough. One has to be diligent. Last, and most important, students must have the wit to be imaginative and to take pride in learning to manipulate the language in order to make it do what they want it to do.

Learning to speak a foreign language, play a musical instrument, or put a basketball through the hoop a hundred times in a row, takes practice, but the rewards are great. Acquiring such skills is an adventure that goes far beyond having fun. It offers the sheer joy and satisfaction that comes with accomplishment. It's part of what makes life worth living.

Ruby Beach, Olympic Peninsula, Washington

The Road to Seattle

If Lake Michigan were not in the way, it would be possible to drive straight west from Detroit, Lansing, and Grand Rapids (all in Michigan) right out to Tomah, Wisconsin, without getting close to Chicago. Because of the lake barrier, however, there is no direct interstate highway link between Detroit and Tomah, so drivers have to go through northern Indiana and Illinois to get there. And when they arrive, they are given the choice which the lake denied them. At Tomah, travelers bound for Seattle can take either a northern (I-94) or a southern (I-90) route for the next part of the trip. Both routes will bring them to Billings, Montana, where the two interstate highways unite as I-90 for the rest of the way to Seattle.

I-90 goes west across southern Minnesota and South Dakota and then heads northwest through some of Wyoming to Billings. I-94 cuts northwest across Minnesota and then goes west through North Dakota into Montana.

Billings is the first of three Montana cities on I-90 that begins with the letter B. The other two are Bozeman and Butte. Billings is the easternmost; Bozeman is in the middle, and Butte is the westernmost. From east to west, the second letters of these cities spell IOU, conveniently providing a tip for those of us who might want some help remembering which city comes when. For children who enjoy looking at maps, it can make the time go a little faster.

After Missoula and St. Regis, the road passes over the Continental Divide and descends to Coeur d'Alene, Idaho. People come here from around the world to enjoy the collision of air from the Pacific Ocean and the northern Great Plains. The locals say it's good for what ails you. The spectacular "Highway in the Sky" leads on toward the border with Washington, the "Apple State."

* * * * * * * *

A few minutes after leaving Idaho, I arrive in Spokane in time for lunch with friends at Mercy Hospital. From here it is more than 150 miles to Ellensburg, which lies 30 miles west of the Columbia River.

This is my first car trip through eastern Washington. Expecting to see apple orchards as I roll along, it comes as a surprise when they don't appear. More than two hours later, the interstate makes a sharp turn to the left, and soon I see the Columbia River far below me. It begins raining hard as I cross the bridge and continue on to Ellensburg. Traffic slows to one lane. It's getting dark, and headlights come into play. The "fast" setting on the windshield wipers makes itself useful. In Ellensburg, the pouring rain turns into heavy, splatting snow, and the traffic slows some more. I stop to fill the car's gas tank. The attendant notices the Minnesota license plate and says, "You're a long way from home, sir."

"Yes, that's true," I say.

"The weather is worse up ahead," he adds, "and it's likely the road to Snoqualmie Pass will be closing."

There is a Safeway store across the street, and I walk over to buy a bottle of Piper-Heidsieck champagne for Herb's New Year's Eve party. Herb, whom I've known for more than fifty years, has offered me the use of his spare bedroom during my visit to the Pacific Northwest. I decide to call him. He tells me there is a storm warning in effect for Snoqualmie and asks if I'll be overnighting in Ellensburg. Spending the night in an unfamiliar place does not appeal to me. I decide to keep going.

Snow is accumulating on the ground, but there's no wind, and the highway is well lit. The snowplows with their yellow beams are at work. An hour passes. The road is crowded with semi-trailer trucks. I'm one car in a long line of cars slowly passing one big rig after another. Their back wheels are spinning – not a good sign. The road is wet and slippery, but clear. Traffic is moving reasonably well, not quite what Minnesotans would call good winter driving conditions, but not really bad either. Halfway between Ellensburg and Snoqualmie Pass, there is an increase in the number of flashing yellow lights. Now and then some blue and red lights from police cars and emergency vehicles are added in. A sign appears: "Snoqualmie Pass, 20 miles." The highway is getting wider; all the lane markings disappear, and soon the road is almost as wide as a football field is long. A huge illuminated signboard announces that chains are now required. The line of cars breaks up, and most of them move off to the right-hand side of the road to get out their chains. The trucks have their own chain-up area farther off in the forest. The whole area is as brightly lit as a Scandinavian Christmas fair.

All at once the cars stop wherever they happen to be, and several dozen police officers swarm around them. I roll down my window and am told to follow the car in front of me to a parking space. I manage to do this without much difficulty. A patrolman waves his flashlight and walks over to my car. He tells me to begin chaining up and moves toward the back of the car, ready to assist me. I follow him and open the trunk. He looks inside and says, "There are no chains in here," and then, with a rather puzzled expression on his face, he turns to me and says, "You don't have any chains."

"No, I don't," is all I can say.

He checks the traffic behind him, sees more cars arriving all the time, pauses for a moment, but before he can put a question together, I say, "I don't need chains. This is a Minnesota car; we know how to drive in snow." The officer's face betrays a trace of surprise. He looks at the license plate, brushes some snow off it, straightens up and says, "Well then, you'd best be getting on your way." With an expansive swoop of his right arm, he waves me on and out of there.

* * * * * * *

The car creeps on toward Snoqualmie Pass. The wind near the top is fierce, and the visibility is worse. It's difficult to see more than a few feet ahead. Just as I'm about to start over the pass in what has turned into a blinding blizzard, the sky and everything around me turns a brilliant shimmering white. Caught in the glare of giant searchlights, I hear what sounds like an airplane. Peering out into the driving snow, I can't believe my eyes: a small plane appears. All its spotlights are on bright, and it's apparently coming in for a landing. It glides over the top of my car, so close I think I can reach up and touch it, but the sun roof is closed.

I make my way down to North Bend where I call Herb to say the weather has cleared, and I can see his house between Green Lake and the University of Washington campus. He laughs. I don't forget to mention the airplane.

Herb says, "Don't worry, take your time. I'll leave the front door unlocked and the porch light on. I've turned down the bed for you." And then he adds, "By the way, just so you know, there is no airport on top of Snoqualmie."

The next day we learn he was wrong about that.

Moses by Michelangelo

February, 2015

One morning sixty years ago, over breakfast, Dad said he was going to Sioux Falls on business later that day and asked if I wanted to go along. He added that as long as he was going there anyway, we might as well stop at Augustana and sign me up for college. That sounded like a good idea. Mother decided to go with us.

When Dad finished his meeting, the three of us went to lunch at the Stockyards Café. Dad always called it the best restaurant in town. From there we drove out to the college. We parked next to Mikkelson Library, near the spot where a copy of Michelangelo's Moses stands today. At the administration building, we spoke with someone at the front desk and told him why we were there. He walked us to President Lawrence Stavig's office and knocked on the door. Dr. Stavig invited us to come in. Dad congratulated him on the football team's winning season. Stavig was pleased and told us how important it is to have a good football team. He said every win means more students for the college. He asked if I played football. Mother said I did not, and added that she and Dad were sending me to Augustana for music.

A year later, my name appeared in the college newspaper as a new member of the a cappella choir. The next day Dr. Stavig stopped me after chapel and asked that I greet my parents for him.

"They must be proud of you," he said.

"Yes, I think they are," I replied.

Stockyards Café, Sioux Falls, c. 1950

* * * * * * * *

"That's how simple it was to get into college in those days," I told my daughter Sagi thirty years later, in 1985, when she was researching colleges.

The catalogs began pouring in even before her junior year in high school. Trying to keep up with them was almost a full-time job for me. When Sagi decided to apply to colleges that were household names throughout the country, I knew we would need some help.

The job didn't get any easier when she said, "You know, choosing the right college is probably one of the most important things a person ever does, kind of like getting married."

Right then and there, I decided to hire a college counselor. After asking around, we learned that one of the best people for the job had taught at Sagi's school and was widely regarded as top-notch. The only question was whether or not she was accepting more clients. (She was.) As the pressure mounted, I felt something like a noose tightening around my neck. If it was going to be an ordeal just finding someone to help Sagi navigate the college application process, how much more difficult would it be to convince a college that she met their expectations? This was clearly a responsibility I could not shoulder alone.

"You wouldn't want me to choose a college that's not a good match and then have me regret it for the rest of my life, would you?" Sagi asked.

I knew at that moment it might not be a matter of life and death, but, at least in our case, it was going to be close.

"No, perish forbid," I answered and gratefully signed the first check for this miracle worker who would take responsibility for my daughter's future happiness, even though that check was written for a sum larger than my first quarter's tuition for graduate school at the University of Chicago in 1964.

The next step was acquainting myself with college rankings, almost an industry in itself. We needed more boxes. Years of information about mutual funds went to recycling. I breathed a big sigh of relief.

No sooner was that accomplished than the matter of deadlines appeared on the horizon. Who could have concocted a system with so many deadlines? Night after night – or so it seems in retrospect – I made trips out to the airport post office just to be sure that envelopes were stamped before the clock struck twelve, never forgetting that all this mail flying out of Minneapolis-St. Paul had to be certified. It also needed tracking numbers, and it included requests for signatures on little green cards that had to be sent back to us by return mail. Just because we had a college counselor working on our behalf did not mean that we were out of the woods where all the denizens of crisis dwell. No, it was one thing after another, a never-ending stream that reminded me of the chocolates on Lucy's conveyor belt in a famous episode of the *I Love Lucy* TV series in the 1950s: they just kept coming.

We had our share of baleful looks, tears, even some slammed doors. Luckily, we escaped shouting matches and screaming fits, but sometimes not by much.

It was a fraught time in our lives, to say the least, a time that tried our souls. Somehow we got through it: letters of recommendation, Xerox copies of our income tax returns, personal essays – they passed over and disappeared into the ether. All that remained was the waiting, probably the most anguishing thing of all.

There was early acceptance, middle acceptance, and regular acceptance. Another special calendar had to be made, and then we tried to settle down a little. Whenever Sagi asked, I had the deadline at my fingertips. What with all the activity, we sometimes almost forgot what the goal was.

I was doing my best, but as everyone knows, one's best is sometimes not good enough. After many repetitions of, "Sorry, Dad, I don't have time to talk with you about that right now," almost all the early acceptance dates had passed. So much for an early end to our agony.

The middle acceptance deadlines were fast approaching: mid-January, early February, mid-February. By paying careful attention, I concluded that the early part of February was the best time to hope for a letter of acceptance.

Thee, Hannah was one of Sagi's favorite books. I wondered if she had mentioned it in an essay, perhaps one to Swarthmore, or Bryn Mawr, where that title has a history. After Swarthmore's acceptance date came and went, I gave up hoping for modest taxi fares between that college campus and the nearby Philadelphia airport. I pinned my hopes on Bryn Mawr, but those hopes were dashed when no letter arrived at the beginning of the second week of February.

With the Quakers out of the picture, I asked Sagi what she expected next. She said Bryn Mawr had been her first choice. When asked what her second – and maybe third – choices were, she dropped a bombshell: she had not made a second or third choice.

"What?" I asked in as calm a voice as I could summon. "How can that be? After all this work, you do not have a back-up choice?"

"No," she answered, "I don't."

My heart went out to her, even though I think it had ceased beating by that time.

"What are we going to do?" passed through my mind, but remained unspoken. I knew it would not be easy to answer that question.

Numb, not saying much, we moved around the room for a while, and then the evening ended. I don't think anyone at our house slept very well that night.

But – miracle of miracles – Bryn Mawr's acceptance letter arrived the next day. The crisis was over. Thirty years had passed since my acceptance at Augustana, and thirty years later I sat down to write this.

Avenue of Trees, Minneapolis

Buffalo

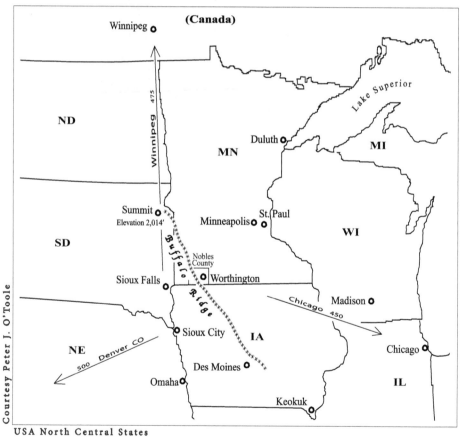

USA North Central States

Addendum

Buffalo Ridge

The early French explorers in the Upper Midwest called the uplands that begin in eastern South Dakota the *Coteaux des Prairies*, the "little hills of the prairie." This region of high ground, a remnant of glacial activity, is 200 to 300 miles long and 50 to 100 miles wide. It covers an area that goes southeast from Summit (elevation 2,014 feet), South Dakota, to Des Moines, Iowa. For more than half that distance, it runs parallel to the Des Moines River which begins at Lake Shetek in Murray County, Minnesota.

People who live in the tri-state area (where South Dakota, Minnesota, and Iowa meet) call it Buffalo Ridge. Those who live on the Ridge and in its environs get their weather news from Sioux Falls, South Dakota, and Sioux City, Iowa. The rain that falls on the west slope of Buffalo Ridge – in the southwesternmost counties of Minnesota – drains via the Rock and Big Sioux rivers into the Missouri River at Sioux City, Iowa. Much of the rainfall on the east slope of the Ridge flows to the Des Moines River and then, losing elevation all the way, it joins the Mississippi River near Keokuk, Iowa.

The crest of Buffalo Ridge was used as a trail by the Native Americans throughout the year; they could follow its southeast diagonal from South Dakota far into Iowa without getting their feet wet. At Worthington, Minnesota, which changed its name from Sioux

271

Crossing in the 1870s, the Buffalo Ridge trail crossed both the East-West trail – Interstate 90 today – and the Southwest diagonal trail that ran from Lake Superior to Denver, Colorado, by way of St. Peter (Minnesota), Sioux City (Iowa), and Kearney (Nebraska).

Here is some thumbnail information about the four southwest Minnesota counties that are sometimes referred to as the "heart" of Buffalo Ridge:

Murray County

Home to mystical Lake Shetek

Nobles County

Borders Iowa and the Ocheyedan (Native American) Mounds

Pipestone County

Home to the Pipestone National Monument, where the sacred ceremonial pipes were made

Rock County

Home of Blue Mounds State Park and a small herd of buffalo

Afterword

Writing down on paper a few of life's happenings can be a rich experience. It has helped me hold close some of the people, places and things that have played important parts in a journey that now covers almost fourscore years.

It is never too late to share with others what we remember. No matter which one of the several arts we choose to employ in this endeavor, it will enhance our understanding of the role we have in life's grand pageant.

Acknowledgments

Lisa Abascal Larson
Monique Bazin
Wayne Beauchemin
Jamie Becker
Estelle Bienhoff
Thomas Blomster
Gordon Boldt
Lester Boots
Audrey Brake
Joyce Broesder
Brenda Bell Brown
Joyce Burk
Jonathan Cain
Tash Casso
Greg Castillo
John Cegielski
Joann Cierniak
Herb Coats
Cindy Cox
Ray Crippen
Mary Davies
Stephanie Deboury
Patrick Demuth
Richard Devlin
Laurie Ebbers
Scott Edelstein
Carolyn Elkin
Germain Elsing
Shawn Elsing
Beverly Engelkes

David Fagerness
Conrad Fisher
Lala Fletcher
Matt Fuerling
Patsy Galstad
Paul Gold
Angie Gowan
Brigitte Guegnaud
Marcel-Paul Guegnaud
William Herrmann
Ken Hershbell
Albert Herzog
Nelly Trocmé Hewett
Kevin Jennings
Leah Kalemba
James Kemp
Alan Knaeble
Janet Larson
Ron Larson
Jodi Lichtor
Darlene Major
Jim Martin
Makoto Matsumoto
Ray Meinders
Sam Miller
Merle Minda
Keith Moheban
Lois Moheban
Norma Nelson
Margaret Odegaard

Baiba Olinger
Jean Peterson
Vali Phillips
Lui Picard
Paul Picard
Alexa Plank
Janice Remmers
Marlene Reuber
Russ Rickers
Jonathan B. Rickert
Théo Schaafsma
Dee Schaefer
Andrew Spannhour
Norton Stillman
Mike Schoberg
John Schoolfield
Warren Schueneman
Bill Sherfey
Janet Shore
LaVonne Johanning Slater
John Slater
Mark Soderbeck
Diane Thome
Jan Thordson
Jennifer Weg
Clint Wolthuizen
Sandy Wood
Chuck Worsinger
Roger Zarn
James Zeese

jessie rennie/Shutterstock.com

Country Dinner Bell

John Elsing

Elsing Farm Garden

In Memoriam

I dedicate this book
to my parents, Mary and Herman,
and my little sister, Marie

Mother was born in Minnesota in 1911 and died here in 2011. She was married to Dad for almost 50 years and lived on his parents' farm for more than 75. Elsing is a Dutch name found in countries bordering the North Sea. It translates as "water meadow." Mother taught school and had two children, Marie and John. Marie taught school in Adrian, and John worked in St. Paul. Mother focused on the farm and its garden, her family and friends, her granddaughters, and great-granddaughter. Five generations of the family are chronicled in John's 2012 book, *Keeping Time: 70 Little Stories*.

John Elsing
Minneapolis
2016

Windmill of Wijk bij Duurstede, Jacob van Ruisdael, 1670

CPSIA information can be obtained
at www.ICGtesting.com
Printed in the USA
BVHW040049271219
567882BV00027B/327/P

9 781546 763956